Workshop in a Workbook...

I0489401

Consultative Selling:
A Model for Sales Success

An Introductory Sales Development Program

This **Consultative Selling** Sales Development Workbook contains nine chapters and seven building blocks for sales success:

Chapter #1 and #2: Consultative Selling: A Model for Sales Success;
Chapter #3: Building Block #1: Call Preparation (Self and Call Preparation);
Chapter #4: Building Block #2: Opening the Call/Making the Connection;
Chapter #5: Building Block #3: Probing and Uncovering Customer Needs;
Chapter #6: Building Block #4: Tailoring a Response/Presentation;
Chapter #7: Building Block #5: Handling Customer Questions/Objections;
Chapter #8: Building Block #6: The A,B,C's of Closing the Sale (or Addressing the Issue); and
Chapter #9: Building Block #7: Follow-Through (Internal and External).

This 91-page resource contains "leading edge" information, which is highly interactive and directly applicable to your role as a Sales Consultant, Account Manager, or Sales Manager. Participants will have an opportunity to understand these concepts and develop skills to contribute to the success experienced by themselves, their teams and the organization. An emphasis is placed on individual and small-group "hands-on" activities which apply and reinforce the concepts. The workbook can be used individually or within sales teams.

Consultative Selling Workbook; V2
www.danduffyauthor.com
©Copyright 2019

"Vision Without Action
Is Just a Dream.
Action Without Vision
Just Passes the Time.
But, Vision and Action
Can Change the World."

Joel Barker, Futurist

"Sales is....Identifying the customers wants and needs, and helping the customer meet those wants and needs."

"Consultative selling is....building long-term business relationships by staying proactive and being solutions oriented."

*The process must benefit both parties, buyer and the seller.
*It considers each person's feelings to be important.
*Focus on we (buyer and seller) and not just me (seller).

Remember: You need the **helping** instinct, not the **killer** instinct.

"Quality Customer Service will give any individual or any organization long term competitive advantage. If you build and support it within the structure of the organization, and nurture and recognize it within the character of the individual, there is no way that this can be duplicated. It becomes an individual's and an organization's competitive advantage." Stephen Covey, Author
Seven Habits of Effective People

Consultative Selling Skills

The What = Quality and Results

The Who = Account Manager and Customer

The How = Skills and Behavioral Flexibility

Program Objectives

-To enhance each Sales Account Managers understanding of Effective Selling, Consultative Selling and the building blocks for sales success,

-To provide an opportunity for Sales Account Manager's to learn and practice concepts by applying them to real "on-the-job" situations in order to strengthen their skills and abilities,and

-To identify and experience the benefits of planning, listening, presenting, handling and closing to increase sales.

Program Chapters

Chapter #1 and #2: Consultative Selling: A Model for Sales Success
Chapter #3: Building Block #1: Call Preparation (Self Preparation and Call Preparation)
Chapter #4: Building Block #2: Opening the Call/Making the Connection
Chapter #5: Building Block #3: Probing and Uncovering Customer Needs
Chapter #6: Building Block #4: Tailoring a Response/Presentation
Chapter #7: Building Block #5: Handling Customer Questions/Objections
Chapter #8: Building Block #6: The A, B, C's of Closing (or Addressing the Issue)
Chapter #9: Building Block #7: Follow-Through (Internal and External)

1. <u>Understand Why the Skill is Important for the Job.</u> Each training and development chapter provides an overview of the topic and its importance. Specific sales situations where the skill can be used, as well as typical "cues" for using the skill, are mentioned. As part of each session, you will discuss how the skill can be used in your role and what the impact could be if the skill was applied.

2. <u>Identify the Key Actions Involved in the Skill.</u> Through individual reading for each chapter and class discussions, you will identify and analyze the steps or Key Actions involved in the successful use of the skill. The rationale for each Key Action, "The Why" will be covered, as well as specific examples, or "The How."

3. <u>See a Demonstration of the Key Actions.</u> For each set of Key Actions, you will see a role play "scenario" demonstration. These demonstrations will show a Account Manager and Customer interaction in a realistic and appropriate manner. These demonstrations are based on realistic situations from your organization. Participants will take notes on these role-play scenarios and will discuss how the Key Actions were used and what effect they had on the interaction. Areas for improvement will also be discussed.

4. <u>Practice the Key Actions. Practice is at the heart of behavior modeling. Practice is</u> required to perfect any skill. Practice builds the skill itself, along with the confidence to apply it to real-time situations.

5. <u>Receive Constructive Feedback on the Use of the Key Actions. Feedback lets individuals</u> know when they have succeeded. Additionally, it also provides someone with information about what aspects of their behavior need to be modified. Participants will receive feedback from fellow participants. This feedback will be based on concrete observation notes taken during individual role-play opportunities.

6. Identify Applications for Key Actions at Work. Individuals will learn about and practice "the rule of three": identifying the skill goals, anticipating obstacles and planning counter-measures in order to apply concepts.

1. Focus on the specific situation, issue or behavior, not on the person. Whether one is talking about child-rearing, supervision, or selling, this principle is key to one's effectiveness in interacting with others. By using this principle, one build's rapport.

2. Demonstrate trust and respect in order to support the self-confidence and self-es -teem of others. Relationships at home and at work are built upon trust and respect. Take the time to treat others *the way they want to be treated* in order to establish a foundation for mutual respect.

3. Strengthen cooperative and constructive relationships with others.
Healthy relationships reduce stress and increase morale which strengthens interdependent work relationships and sales relationships.

4. Never underestimate the power of effective communication and teamwork. Two-way communication and teamwork go hand-in-hand. Communication and teamwork are essential to success for all high performing sports and organizational teams. Open communication also strengthens customer confidence and loyalty.

5. Lead by example and take initiative to make things happen.
"Just Do It!" By taking initiative and leading by example you are able to demonstrate to others in your organization, and to your customers, what is important to you. This behavior provides "value-added" benefits, in the eyes of your customers, which differentiates you from the competition.

6. Obtain the information first, by asking open-ended questions.
In order to provide consultative services, a sales person needs to understand the customer's situation "from the customer's perspective." By asking a series of open-ended questions, a sales person creates a non-judgemental environment for obtaining the information they need.

7. Understand why personal styles and preferences require behavioral flexibility. As human beings, we share one thing in common. We are all unique! Understanding the personal styles and preferences of ourselves and others provides us with the ability to adjust our style and preference to "match" that of another. As a result of this behavioral flexibility, we all ow an individual to remain in their comfort zone. And when comfort levels increase, so does their ability to cooperate.

Chapter One

Sales Skills Training

Welcome to sales training! Whether you are an experienced sales professional, a newcomer to sales, or work in a sales support function, there is always something you can do to sharpen your skills, and that's what this training is all about. The purpose of this training is to learn, or perhaps reinforce some basic principles of sales technique. We're going to cover various aspects of the sales call, which can be viewed from both an inbound and an outbound perspective. These include: effective call preparation, good questioning techniques, handling objections, and many other topics. This training will be useful and informative for anyone who desires to enhance their sales skills and should also be helpful for those who aspire to be promoted. Whether you are new to the organization, or are an experienced sales associate, it is anticipated that this training will provide you with a fresh perspective.

It has been said that there is no such thing as an excellent organization, only those that believe in continuous improvement. We'd like to view this concept on an individual level, by suggesting that there is no such thing as the "perfect" salesperson, only those who believe in continuous improvement.

Just think for a moment, each one of us has specific skills, abilities, resources, and experiences. And, where we are now, in terms of what we are achieving, is the direct result of our past preparation, development, skills, and commitment.

Kaizen: Continuous Improvement
Making incremental improvements, doing "little things" better;
setting and achieving ever higher standards of performance.

The idea of continuous improvement simply means that we can always learn to do something better, more productively, more profitably, and the key to obtaining these type of results is for us to be...
- open,
- ready to learn,
- capable of sharing,
- willing to change and
- able to adapt how we conduct ourselves.

We are anticipating that this training will provide you with the opportunity to share and shape secrets of personal success within the group. Working together and sharing ideas is the best way to both learn and to help yourself to become the superior sales professional that you know you can be! So let's get started by examining a formula for your sales success......

> ## Skills + Activities =Performance

This formula is quite simple. The **Skills** portion refers to the abilities, techniques and competencies that each one of us has as a sale professional. The **Activities** portion of the formula refers to both each sales associate's and their sales manager's visible observable actions or practices in applying their skills to their day-to-day challenges and responsibilities. And the **Performance** segment of the equation refers to the results that both sales associates, sales managers, sales teams and the organization achieves.

What are some examples of <u>skills that you currently have</u> and activities which you currently <u>demonstrate</u> which significantly influence your performance?

- My Strengths: _____

- My Areas for Improvement: _____

*How satisfied are you with your current level of skills, activities and your performance?

> **What is the single most important ingredient to your sales success?**

The Five Elements of the Sales Process

The sales process can be summarized into five essential elements, each of which have to be present during a sales associates interactions with a customer in order for the contact to be considered **a sales contact *and not a social contact.*** These elements are as follows: Planning, Listening, Presenting, Handling, and Closing. Let's define them individually and outline how the Sales Skill Training resources will relate to each of the five elements.

Planning: It has been said that "opportunity is where preparation meets challenge" and the initial planning process plays a significant role in your foundation for success.

1. It allows you to be thorough and include all points necessary to make a good presentation—such things as benefits, customer information, possible objections and closes.

2. Because you are prepared you feel more confident. This confidence is passed on through your voice. Subtle, but different, inflections and tones send out the message of "confidence."

3. Because you are more confident, your customer notices automatically, believes your presentation more, and is more likely to buy your product or service.

Building Block #1: Call Preparation of Sales Training includes the following planning information.
1. Adapting Your Attitude
2. Self-Esteem
3. Avoiding Negativity
4. Self-Talk/Affirmations
5. Readiness/Success Model
6. Planning Your Approach
7. Prospecting Preparation
8. Qualifying Your Prospects
9. Handling Rejection

What are the benefits to you and your customer of Planning & Call Preparation?

Listening: Effective communication begins with focused listening for understanding. We truly can't say we understand the customer's perspective without first taking the time and concentration to listen to what they have to say. By truly listening, you are building that unspoken bond between you and your customer. We've all been around a person who talked constantly and never listened. Generally, we can't wait to get away. If you are doing this with your customers, they will react the same way. It's also important to put some "body language" into your phone conversations, such as saying, "un huh," or "I see."

> **Why is Listening to customer needs, as well as communicating your understanding and reinforcement of their message, a must for successful sales professionals?**

Building Block #2: Opening The Call/Making The Connection of Sales Training includes the following listening and communications information.

10. Establishing the Purpose of the Call
11. Telephone Skills/Etiquette
12. First Impressions
13. Speaking the Prospect's Language

> **What is meant by "Making the Connection" and can a call be considered a success if you made the connection with a customer's voice mail?**

Building Block #3: Probing and Uncovering Customer Needs of Sales Training also includes the following listening and communications information.

14. Asking Open-Ended Questions
15. Listening for Understanding
16. Managing Distractions/Self Discipline
17. Responding with Decisiveness

> **Why is the skillful use of open-ended questioning techniques important in Consultative Selling and how can you strengthen your ability in this area?**

Presenting: Because presentation skills strengthen your ability to provide solutions for your customer, they are extremely important to your success as a sales professional. Presenting needs to satisfy your customer in several ways. You must be able to present your product or service in terms of how they will best help your customer. That's what they are interested in. Equally important, you have the chance to confirm that your information is correct which helps prevent such disasters as providing them with the wrong product, billing at the wrong address, etc. Finally, successful presenting permits you to build a justifiable business case for your customer. In other words, your presentation will provide them with both the economic information as well as the overall justification for their purchase.

Although individuals make many decisions emotionally, our customers have to know, and you have to show, *how your product or service will help their business*—in **dollars and "sense" (justifying the purchase.)**

> **What are several ways in which you can demonstrate to your customers how your products and services will assist their business in dollars and "sense"?**

Building Block #4: Tailoring a Response or Sales Presentation of Sales Training includes the following presenting information.

18. You and Your Customer's Style

19. Special Effects/Adding Impact (Pauses, Analogies, Humor, Drama)
20. Sell the Customer on Benefits/Advantages
21. Solution Oriented Sales

> **Why is it important to identify "and match" through behavioral flexibility, a custom -er's style of communicating? Identify an example of this behavior?**
>
> **Why is it important to communicate product features AND customer benefits?**
>
> **What is meant by solution oriented or "total solution" sales? Identify an example.**

Handling Objections: Addressing or answering customer questions and/or objections is a natural part of the sales process. There are many ways that objections are phrased, yet they all boil down to a few key types. By doing some preparation ahead of time, you will be better prepared to handle those objections calmly and effectively—something that often separates successes from failures. Understanding that objections are not personal attacks and, in fact good signs, allows you to preserve your positive attitude (which is crucial to your success). After all, if your customers have objections, that proves they're listening to you. Right?

Building Block #5: Handling Customer Objections of Sales Training includes the following information on handling objections.

22. Provide Clarification of Information
23. Dealing with Time Delays/Stalling
24. Price Objections
25. Questioning Techniques

Why is it important for a sales associate to understand the difference between a customer's statements, questions and objections?

Closing: Closing is often one of the areas most neglected in sales. However, if the above four elements of planning, listening, presenting, and handling objections are addressed consistently by the sales associate, then closing will be the inevitable outcome of each customer contact. An effective sales presentation must have several places where the sales associate can attempt to close the sale. To succeed, you need to be able to identify opportunities, have a planned close and ask when the opportunity arises.

Building Block #6 The A, B, C's of Closing the Sale of Sales Training includes the following information on closing.

26. Putting It All Together
27. Always Be Closing
28. Closing "Moment's of Truth"
29. Asking for the Order
30. Keep Closing/Add On Sales
31. Understanding Customer's Buying Signals

Building Block #7 Follow-Through and Begin Again of Sales Training includes the following information on closing.

32. Thanking the Customer
33. Sales is Service....Service is Sales
34. Address Issues Promptly
35. Reinforce Sales Consultant Role
36. Ask for Referrals

Now that you have a basic understanding of the five elements of the sales process, think about both your skills and activities within each of the five areas and rate yourself below on a Scale of 1 (I need improvement) to 10 (I am a role model.)

	SKILLS (The What)	ACTIVITIES (The How)
1. Planning	_____	_____
2. Listening	_____	_____
3. Presenting	_____	_____
4. Handling	_____	_____
5. Closing	_____	_____

After each participant has completed their personal ratings of their skills and activities within each of the categories of Planning, Listening, Presenting, Handling, and Closing, have a group discussion on the following:

A. Which of the five elements do you think is most important in order for a sales associate to be as effective and successful as possible in the eyes of the customer?

B. Which of the five elements do you think is most important in order for a sales associate to be as effective and successful as possible in the eyes of the organization?

C. If you were to prioritize each of the above five elements from #1 - #5 in order of importance.....what order would you put them in?

D. Which of the elements are you most in need of improvement in and why?

E. Which of the elements are you most effective in and why?

Market Connected

Action Oriented

Absolute Results Oriented

Willingness to be Coached

Team Oriented

Empowered People

Open, Honest Communications

Organization Reflection and Learning

Loyal, Discreet and Confidential

Market Connected - The Sales Associate understands and knows the market and market prices and the economic viability of their customer base. In addition, the Sales Associate positions himself/herself as a solution provider for each customer, building a strategic partnership between the organization and the account. In addition market resources, including appropriate trade journals, are read and reviewed weekly.

Action Oriented - The Sales Associate takes initiative to complete tasks in a timely manner and is proactive in resolving customer issues.

Absolute Results Oriented - Accountable for individual monthly gross profit plan and goals. Maintain company performance expectations for activities (phone time, new accounts, prospecting number of orders, and account penetration).

Willingness To Be Coached - The Sales Associate takes direction well and displays a positive attitude in all facets of the business.

Team Oriented - Works with other people in a positive and professional environment strategizing and problem solving business issues that may arise.

Empowered People - Is a self-starter ("take the ball and run" with it attitude), believes in themself and their individual contribution to the organization.

Open, Honest Communication- Two-Way Communication at all times.

Organization Reflection and Learning- When a mistake is made, understands why the mistake was made and reflects back on the steps that caused the error. Learns from their experience so it does not happen again.

Loyal, Discreet and Confidential- This is a must to establish and preserve credibility.

Why are the above dimensions of success important to a sales professional?

Chapter Two

Effective Selling: A Model for Sales Success

The **Effective Selling Model** provides a sales person with a practical way to create sales and build the rapport necessary for strong and enduring customer relationships. The model is both tactical and strategic. By understanding and applying the Effective Selling Model, you can develop the competencies necessary to **be a true professional in a world that wants to buy and not be sold**. It is important to remember that these selling styles are *behaviors* and that the Effective Selling Model is a *behavioral* model. Selling Styles should be appropriate to the Buying Willingness levels of the prospect or customer to maximize effectiveness.

Mind Set X to Mind Set Y

Salespeople enter customer interactions from one of two-value sets...Mind Set X or Mind Set Y:

•Those driven by **Mind Set X** values base their behaviors on the attitude— "I must make the sale no matter what......I must make the sale at any cost."

• **Mind Set Y** salespeople approach selling with—"I'm here to help the customer solve problems and satisfy their needs....If I focus on the needs of the customer, then I will have my needs met, too."

What strategies might a sales professional use to avoid Mind Set X *behavior*?

What would indicate that a sales professional was using a Mind Set Y approach?

A salesperson's values affect the way that they come across in their interactions with customers. People with Mind Set X and Y are perceived in the following way:

MIND SET X	MIND SET Y
•Concern for self	•Concern for customers
•Hard sell	•Soft sell
•Canned presentations	•Questions and discussion
•Talking	•Listening
•Pushing product	•Providing opportunity to buy
•Presenting features	•Providing benefits
•Advocating product without acknowledging	•Identifying needs/benefits

Mind Set Y is the foundation of **Effective Selling**. It focuses on *customer* needs, not the needs of the salesperson. This is essential in an era of increasing customer education and sophistication. Rather than "making the sale," it is important to provide customers *with an opportunity to buy*. This helps develop the long-term relationships that are so necessary to the sales process.

Selling Styles

In the Effective Selling model, there are two dimensions of behavior that make up selling styles: *product (or service) focus* and *supportive focus*. Each of these is associated with its respective dimension in the Effective Leadership model:

•**Product Focus** represents *task behavior*. It is the extent to which a salesperson provides the what, how, when, where, and who to customers.

•**Supportive Focus** represents *relationship behavior*. It is the extent to which a salesperson engages in two-way or interactive communication. The behaviors include listening, encouraging, facilitating and problem-solving.

What are some examples of Product Focus and Supportive Focus?

Keep in mind that each dimension of the Effective Selling model is a continuum from low to high. The different combinations of Product Focus and Supportive Focus can be divided into quadrants that represent the *four fundamental selling styles (FS1, FS2, FS3, and FS4)*.

Selling Behaviors

High	Presenting	Probing
	Enhancing needs. Asking for the sale. Responding to questions/objections. **FS3** Hi Support/Lo Product	Question to gain insight. Encourage, guide and advocate. **FS2** Hi Product/Hi Support
	Satisfying Following up & through Expanding business. Responding to issues. **FS4** Low Support/Lo Product	**Connecting** Provide specific inform-ation and state purpose of the call. **FS1** Hi Product/Lo Support

Supportive Focus (vertical axis label, High to Low)

Low — Product Focus — High

Selling Phases

FS1 and FS2: **Prospecting** to identify potential need/resources.

FS2 and FS3: **Handling and Closing** to ensure sales success.

FS3 and FS4: **Servicing** to support long term sales relationships.

Because the Effective Selling model is a behavioral model, it represents a variety of visible observable actions that a salesperson can display based on the willingness of the buyer. Buyer Willingness of a prospect or customer is affected by--*knowledge of* and *commitment to*--a number of factors.   They include:

> • **The product or service.** People need a computer and software to perform their specific job. They have a certain amount of knowledge about computers and software and are committed to purchasing.

> •**The company or organization.** Some people are committed to computers or software manufactured (or sold) by a particular company. They buy from that company when they have a need.

> •**The brand or model.** Some people are knowledgeable about and committed to specific BRANDS or MODELS. In some cases, they may not remember the name of the company that manufactures "their" brand or model.

> • **The salesperson.** Some people have been known to buy products from a particular salesperson. But, when the salesperson goes to another company, the customers follow. Their commitment and loyalty is to the salesperson.

Buyer Willingness: The product knowledge and product commitment continuum of buying willingness can be divided into four ranges, BW1, BW2, BW3, and BW4.

•**Buyer Willingness Level 1: (BW1) Uninformed/Uncommitted**
(ie: "I don't know that much about your product or company.")

•**Buyer Willingness Level 2: (BW2) Uninformed/Interested**
(ie: "Sounds interesting, but I need more details about how it can help my situation.)

•**Buyer Willingness Level 3: (BW3) Knowledgeable/Apprehensive**
(ie: "I can see how this could be helpful but I need to think about it.")

•**Buyer Willingness Level 4: (BW4) Knowledgeable/Committed**
(ie: "We have had success using your product and would recommend it to others.")

High

Supportive Focus

Presenting	Probing
Enhancing needs. Asking for the sale. Responding to questions/objections.	Question to gain insight. Encourage, guide and advocate.
FS3	**FS2**
Hi Support/Lo Product	Hi Product/Hi Support
Satisfying	Connecting
Following up & through. Expanding business. Responding to issues.	Provide specific inform-ation and state purpose of the call.
FS4	**FS1**
Lo Support/Lo Product	Hi Product/Lo Support

Low   Product Focus   High

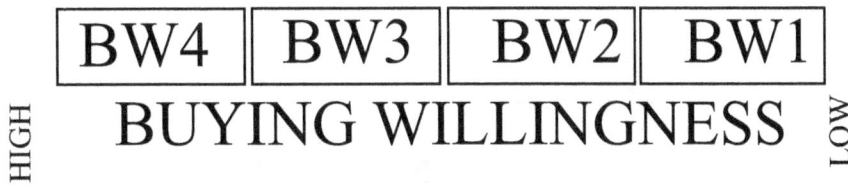

BW4	BW3	BW2	BW1

HIGH   **BUYING WILLINGNESS**   LOW

- •Buyer Willingness Level 1: (BW1) Uninformed/Uncommitted
- •Buyer Willingness Level 2: (BW2) Uninformed/Interested
- •Buyer Willingness Level 3: (BW3) Knowledgeable/Apprehensive
- •Buyer Willingness Level 4: (BW4) Knowledgeable/Committed

This Effective Selling Application Exercise is designed to provide participants with an opportunity to use the Effective Selling Model as a framework for creating opening benefits statements for both initial and follow-up calls. The exercise will also allow participants to identify benefits of doing business with the company and using it's products and services.

Exercise: You and another sales person will team up to complete this exercise. You both will review the following situations and complete the information requested as it relates to how you would approach both an initial call and a follow up call with a prospect.

Initial Call/Contact Situation:

1. Prospect Buying Willingness is BW1: Uninformed/Uncommitted

2. Appropriate Effective Selling Salesperson Behavior
   is... •Provide information on....salesperson, company and products/services.
   •State the Purpose of the Call...
   •Provide prospect with the benefits to them...
   •Ask a transitional question...

3. Create an Opening Benefit Statement... "Why should a prospect listen to me?"
   A. Explore with your teammate the benefits of doing business with you and your organization. Identify at least six "value-added" benefits which can be of assistance to your prospects AND differentiate you and your company from the competition.

1.	**4.**
2.	**5.**
3.	**6.**

4. Using the above benefits, role play an initial call with a prospect using the benefits as part of an opening benefit statement. Also, ask your prospect a "transitional question" which encourages their response and involvement in the discussion and moves the prospect toward BW2 buyer willingness.

Follow Up Call Situation:

1. Prospect Buying Willingness is still BW1: Uninformed/Uncommitted

2. Appropriate Effective Selling Salesperson Behavior is...
> •Provide information on....salesperson, company and
> products/services.
> •State the Purpose of the Call...
> •Provide prospect with the benefits to them...
> •Ask a transitional question...

3. Create an Opening Benefit Statement..."Why should a prospect listen to me?"

> **B. Explore with your teammate the benefits of the _____ (fill-in the blank) specialty product or service line available through your organization...**

> **C. Explore with your teammate the benefits of _____ (another specialty product/service line) available through your organization.**

> **D. Explore with your teammate the benefits of _____ (another specialty product/service line) available through your organization.**

> **For either B, C or D, above, identify at least six "value-added" benefits of this product line which can be of assistance to your prospects AND differentiate you and your company from the competition.**

> 1.   4.
> 2.   5.
> 3.   6.

4. Using one of the above benefits (A, B, C, or D), role play a follow up call with a prospect using the benefits as part of a benefit statement based on a need you uncovered. Also, ask your prospect a "transitional question" which continues their response and involvement in the discussion and moves the prospect closer to BW2 buyer willingness.

Chapter Three

Building Block #1: Call Preparation

> When people fail at many different things.... "They always have an excuse."
> When a few succeed...... "They always have a plan."

It has been said that one minute of planning saves three minutes of execution. This certainly applies to sales and helps you create more sales. Without a plan, you're not sure what you're trying to do, how you are going to do it, or what options you have. What's worse is that's the way you sound to your customer—confused. Very few sales are made this way. By planning your call, you not only feel more confident in your presentation but you sound more confident. Before you pick up the phone, whether it is for an inbound or an outbound call, you need to prepare yourself emotionally, attitudinally and strategically.....to be the most effective you can be for yourself, your customer and your organization.

Before you can ever think of picking up a phone to answer or make a call, you must be prepared. You must:

A. Develop an I-Can-Do-Attitude: Stay positive. Stay upbeat. You are your own greatest asset; focusing on negatives keeps you from performing at your peak. In Stephan Shiffman's book <u>The Twenty Five Most Common Sales Mistakes, he says that in his</u> work with many salespeople, he has come to the conclusion that there are some people who simply spend their whole careers inventing and/or reinforcing obstacles.

•〉 Do you agree or disagree with this statement?
•〉 List examples of this type of behavior in a work environment?
•〉 How can you alter or prevent it from happening in the first place?

B. Avoid Negativity:

•⟩ Explore "the wrong side of the bed" syndrome. Why some days start out lousy and get worse.

•⟩ Why people who take things too personally are more prone to negativity.

•⟩ "Pebble in the pond" - The far reaching effects of an ugly disposition.

C. Enhance Your Self Esteem: - Feel Good About Yourself:

•⟩ Why is self-esteem so important for success in sales?

•⟩ Is there a direct or indirect correlation between self-esteem and negativism? And why would elevating one of them (ie: self-esteem or negativism) eliminate or counteract the other?

•⟩ A person with healthy self-esteem doesn't have to prove themselves to themselves or to anyone else. Instead, they wonder how many people they will be able to help each day with the products or services they're selling.

•⟩ Sales professionals with high esteem are not self-centered. As a result, they focus their attention on customers and constantly look for ways to build rapport and make customers feel comfortable throughout the conversation.

D. Engage in Creative Visualization, Self-Talk and Affirmations:

What are some examples of self-talk that are Pro or Con?
What impact do positive or negative words play in them?
What are some examples of self-talk and affirmations that you use?
And what is the benefit of engaging in positive self-talk and affirmations?

Four Basic Steps for Effective Creative Visualization
1. Set your goal.
2. Create a clear picture of it.
3. Focus on it often.
4. Give it positive energy.

Affirmations

To affirm means "to make firm." An affirmation is a strong, positive statement that some thing is already so. It is a way of "making firm" that which you are imaging.

The practice of engaging in affirmations allows us to begin replacing some of our stale, worn out, or negative mind chatter with more positive ideas and concepts. It is a powerful technique, one which can in a short time transform many of our attitudes and expectations about life, and thereby help to change what we create for ourselves.

Affirmations can be done silently, spoken aloud, written down, or even sung or chanted. Even ten minutes a day of repeating effective affirmations can counterbalance years of old mental habits. An affirmation can be any positive statement. Here are a few sales related affirmations just to give you ideas:

•I begin each day with a clear mind and a specific plan to get the most from my time, my effort. I follow my plan and I reach my goals.

•I am always prepared. I take the time to do it right. In everything I do, I am prepared, confident, self-assured, and successful.

•I always take care of the details in my work. I enjoy the details of selling and I always tend to them on time and with full attention.

•I keep myself "up." I know that making good sales presentations means keeping myself up, energetic, and in control. That is exactly the way I am, and my sales presentations are always professional and effective.

•I never avoid addressing an issue or making a sales call of any kind. I keep myself working and that keeps me winning.

E. Gauge Your Readiness and Envision a Success Model:
•〉 Do I have the necessary sales skills to excel?
•〉 Am I familiar with all the requirements of my role?
•〉 Do I know what the measurement criteria are which tells me when I'm doing a good job?
•〉 Do I have a plan and practiced techniques which I consistently follow for....
  -Territory Analysis and Profiling
    -Pre-Call Planning and Qualifying
    -The 1st Cold Call (Present Your Case), The 2nd Call (Refer to Offer),
    -The 3rd Call (To Make Progress) and The Follow-Up Call (We're Here to Serve)

F. Plan Your Outbound Approach:

•⟩ To help prepare, try answering the following questions...

1. What do I already know about my territory?
2. What tools can I use to research this territory?
3. What kind of information am I looking for?

4. Is this a brand new territory? If so, let's discuss the significance of this, including how and why you would approach things differently.

5. What are my major money making accounts, top ten, top twenty? Let's discuss why this information is significant to you as an Account Executive.

6. From the information supplied to me, can I determine who my prospecting accounts will be? Discuss what some good methods are for making these determinations.

7. What is my sales target for this month?
8. Do I know how, when, and why I should match price or discount?

9. Do I know how to prioritize my day so I will be able to develop a daily plan?

10. Have I set goals and am I monitoring my progress toward achieving them?

> **Am I Reaching Enough New/Existing Prospects, Qualifying & Profiling Them?**

G. Prepare for Resistance and Rejection:

Sometimes, no matter how hard you prepare, you will encounter resistance when calling. Don't let it discourage you. It is not a personal rejection, it's a business refusal. It means that the prospect may not have enough information to justify buying, or the need isn't there, or the money isn't there. It does not mean you aren't a good person or a good Account Executive.

Don't get angry if the customer doesn't want to give you all the information immediately. There may also be many reasons why your customer doesn't buy when you want him to.

It's your job to find out why he doesn't buy, and to try to show the value of purchasing your products and services. The reality is that nobody closes every sale.(It is important though to analyze why your prospect hasn't bought after several conversations.) Remember, if you get angry or upset, you seriously hurt your chances for closing future sales. Control your feelings and emotions—as you will have another chance at it. Stay positive, plan your work, work your plan and win the next one.

Chapter Four

Building Block #2: Opening the Call.

The successful Account Executive knows that it is impossible to succeed in sales without good communication skills. Since the telephone takes away a key communication tool (your eyes), you have to replace it with verbal substitutes. Equally important, you have to make sure you really understand what your customer is saying. Remember these important facts when you are communicating with prospects/customers:

- Most decisions are made using emotions rather than logic.
- People's perceptions are real to them.
- The more you get someone to talk, the smarter *you* appear to them.
- Effective Communication/Listening Skills have to be practiced.

> **"Communication is the use of words and other symbols to achieve various outcomes"**

Personal Communication Styles

A. List three of your best communication qualities. (Continue Doing These...)

B. List three communication qualities that you don't have now but would like to have. (Start Doing These...)

C. List three of your behaviors that block effective communication. (Stop Doing These...)

> *Through Effective Communication, the sender and the receiver both share responsibility for mutual understanding*

SENDER

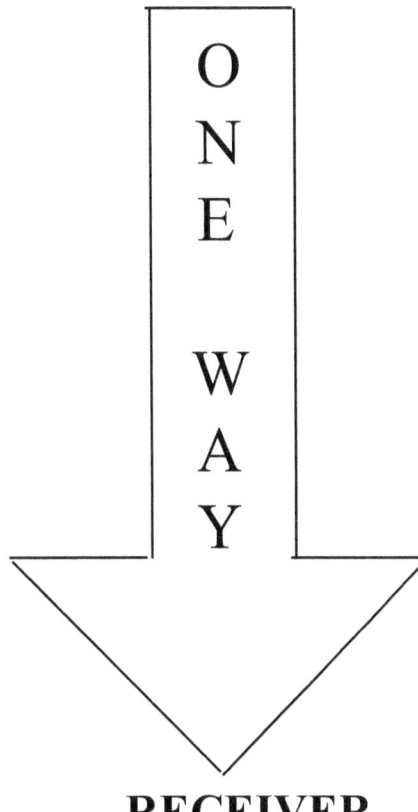

RECEIVER

Linear or one way communication involves only one speaker and one or more listeners. The speaker is usually giving information or directions. This type of communication is effective in situations which require no discussion, no feedback.

List some examples of how linear communication is used in Consultative Sales:

1.
2.
3.

Advantages of linear communication:

1.
2.
3.
4.

Disadvantages of linear communication:

1.
2.
3.
4.

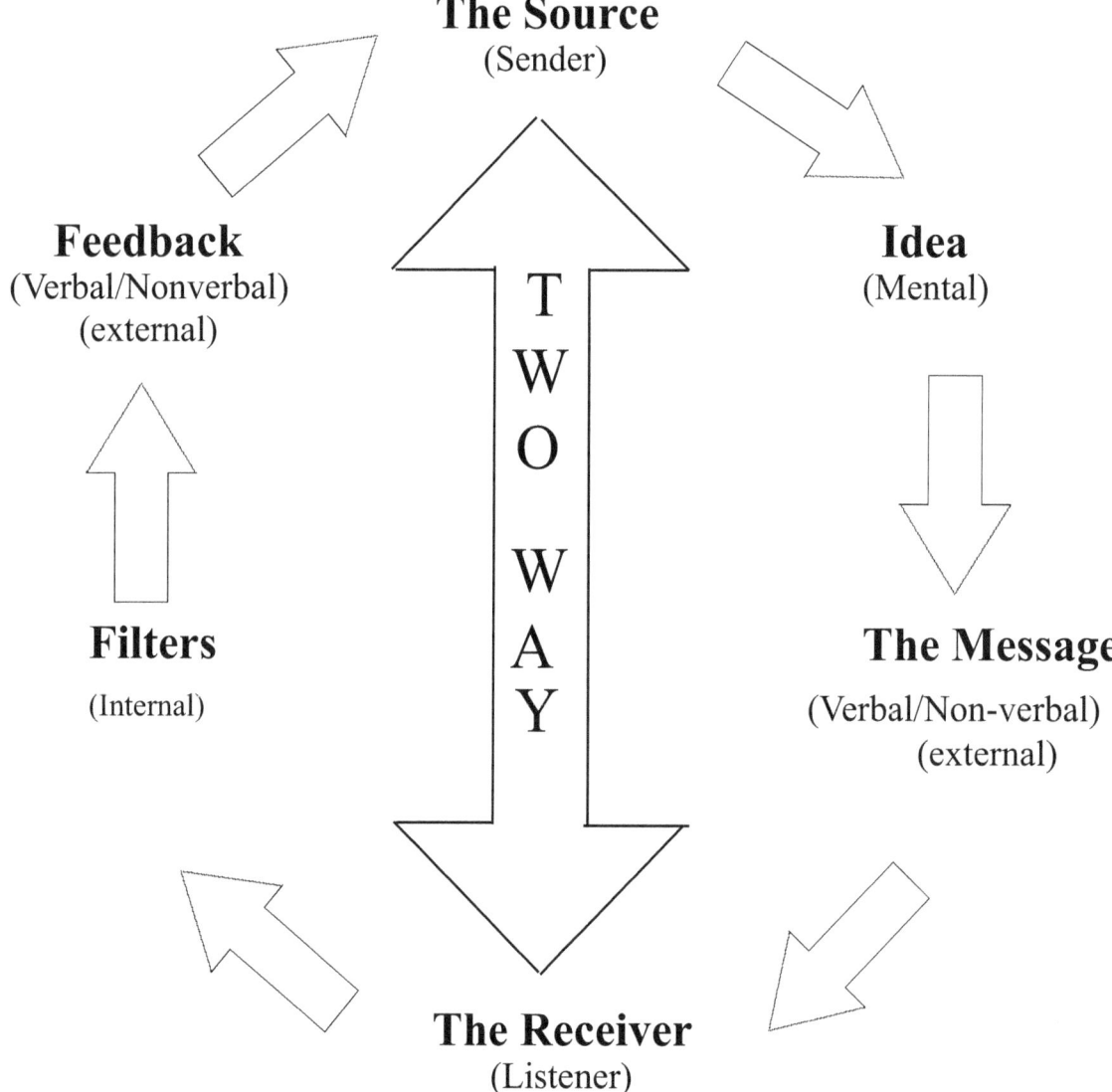

The Source
(Sender)

Feedback
(Verbal/Nonverbal)
(external)

T
W
O

W
A
Y

Idea
(Mental)

Filters

(Internal)

The Message

(Verbal/Non-verbal)
(external)

The Receiver
(Listener)

*In this model, communication is viewed as dynamic and interactive-The path of communication is circular as each element is set in motion and the process ends where it started.

*The external, visible, observable actions are focused on the interaction between the **SENDER** (source) and the **RECEIVER** (listener). However, the source or sender begins the exchange as a result of an internal process of an **IDEA MESSAGE** (words, gestures, tone of voice, and perhaps visual aids).

*The **MESSAGE** travels through a medium or means of communication to the **RECEIVER** (listener).

*The next step in the communication process is when the Recipient of this message internally processes the message by making meaning from the information and extracting value from ideas.

***FILTERS**, internal to each individual, are important at this stage because they can both assist or impede communication. Because filters "screen" how we perceive a message, they can unconsciously reinforce our existing thoughts/views which may prevent us from viewing people, an event, or concept more objectively.

Examples of filters (preconceived ideas and perceptions include:

-Emotional Feelings	-Age
-Economic Status	-Cultural Background
-Gender	-Language
-Education	-Life Experiences

***FEEDBACK**, both verbal and non-verbal, is the receivers external, visible observable actions which are designed to demonstrate the listener's ability to hear, understand, evaluate, and respond to the sender's idea. This phase generally allows the listener to become the speaker and the cycle continues.

Communicate Quality

IN BUSINESS, ABSENCE.... *doesn't make the heart grow fonder.*
No news isn't good news. Business relationships thrive on constant communications - communications that will be all the more effective if they're planned, conducted, checked, and reviewed in keeping with an underlying quality imperative.

What kind of quality messages are you really sending to your customers?

Interpersonal communication can be defined as communication involving two or more people in which each takes turns being the speaker and the listener. The listener understands the **meaning** of what the speaker said. **Both** the listener and the speaker have to work together effectively to make sure this happens.

List some examples of how interactive communication is used in Consultative Sales?

1.

2.

3.

Advantages of interactive communication:

1.

2.

3.

Disadvantages of interactive communication:

1.

2.

3.

Effective communication depends upon two people working together.

Many people approach communication as though it were the simple process of one person telling something to another.

"The ability to express an idea is as important as the idea itself"
Bernard Baruch

According to professor Albert Mehrabian of UCLA, one of the foremost experts in personal communications, there are three elements that comprise communication: the **verbal** which is the message itself, the words you say; the **vocal** which is the intonation, projection and resonance of the voice that carries those words; and the **visual** element which is what people see of your face and your body.

The key ingredient to effective communicating is BELIEVABILITY!

Telephone Skills: How you sound influences your customers perception of you.

Voice Volume - Your voice volume should be the same as if you were talking to someone across the table from you (@3-5 feet).

Rate of Speech - Rate of speech varies depending on what part of the country you're from, but you should try to average 180 words per minute. If you are too slow, prospects and customers get bored. If you are too fast, they can't understand and get frustrated.

Tone/Pitch - Although very difficult to determine, tone can be a real asset or liability. If you say "Uh Hum" in your regular volume, that will be close to the tone and pitch you should use. Have an honest friend give you feedback on your tone.

Voice/Vocal Variety - Your voice transmits energy. Your vocal tone and quality can count for much of "Your Message." Use vocal variety and stay clear of a monotone. Emphasize the   right word.

Articulation-The following areas all deal with improving speech.
•Posture   •Voice Obstacles   •Slang   •Technical Jargon •Non-Words

Listener Involvement - ...To maintain the active interest and involvement of each person with whom you are communicating, every time you talk--whether one person or one thousand.

Dress/Appearance - The most important two words for effective dress are **"be appropriate."**

Effective Telephone Techniques:

1. Smile
2. Speak clearly and concisely.
3. Be enthusiastic.
4. Lower your voice pitch.
5. Talk in positives.
6. Be prepared for questions and objections.
7. Talk directly into the mouth piece of the handset.
8. Consider your customer's personality (Style preference)
9. Speak in terms of benefits. (Customer: Why is that important to me? So What?)
10. Discuss rather than tell.
11. Always thank the listener for their time.
12. Follow-Up and Follow-Through.

Ineffective Telephone Techniques:

1. Frown.
2. Mumble.
3. Sound tired.
4. Speak in a monotone.
5. Be negative.
6. Be overconfident.
7. Hold the telephone handset under your chin.
8. Ramble.
9. Argue.
10. Hang up abruptly.
11. Forget to thank the listener.
12. Try to talk and do something else at the same time.

Unspoken Expectations - Assumptions based on past experience.

Prejudgments - When we come to a decision without fully understanding the facts.

Self-Fulfilling Prophecies - When you "tell" yourself what the outcome of a situation will be   before it happens.

People hear only 25% of what we say:

We hear at a rate of 150 words per minute
Our brain processes at a rate of 600 words per minute

Verbal Cues which reveal Customer's Perceptions - Experts in the field of neurolinguistics have concluded that people express themselves in terms of how they perceive the world--and according to which senses affect them most strongly. Before you can understand how you can adapt your listening style to communicate better, you need to examine some typical examples which fall within the following three categories: Visual, Auditory and Kinesthetic.

Visual: Prospects and Customers with a strong visual orientation might respond to your suggestion by saying:

"I see your point."   "I can envision that."

"That looks good to me."   "I can't get clear on what you mean."

"I think your reasonings fuzzy."   "I don't understand your focus."

Auditory: Prospects and Customers who favor a strong auditory orientation might respond in the following ways:

"I hear you."   "What I hear doesn't impress me."

"It comes through loud and clear."   "I'm not tuned into this idea."

"Sounds good/Doesn't sound good to me."   "It's too complicated."

Kinesthetic: Prospects and Customers who favor a strong kinesthetic orientation rely on "gut feelings," sensation and sensory learning and might say things like:

"I feel good about that."   "That feels right."

"I have a gut feeling about that."   "I don't feel like that the right approach."

VISUAL	AUDITORY	KINESTHETIC
___A. Puts equipment together using printed directions.	___A. Has someone else read directions when putting together equipment.	___A. Puts equipment together using sense of touch.
___B. Frequently makes, uses, and relies on daily "lists".	___B. Plans daily schedule by "talking it through" with someone else.	___B. No schedule. Prefers action to structure.
___C. When in a strange city, prefers to get map and find own way.	___C. When in a strange city, prefers to stop and ask for directions.	___C. When in a strange city, prefers to keep driving as long as possible and "feel the way."
___D. Reads/writes in spare time.	___D. Listens to music in spare time.	___D. Uses spare time for physical activites and keeping fit.
___E. Communicates best by writing.	___E. Communicates best by talking.	___E. Gestures are a critical part of communication style.

The Personal Style Survey is a selected list of statements that describes visible and observable actions of people in relation to their preferences for Directness, Indirect -ness, People, and Task.

By completing a Personal Style survey, you will be able to determine your Style & The Style of others.

	Indirect	Direct
Task	Analyzer	Director
People	Relater	Socializer/ Influencer

"People have one thing in common; We are all different."

People have one thing in common: they are all different"
Robert Zend

Check one word from each pair, responding to the statement, "If I were forced to choose, I would say...I am..." Think of your role within the company and pick the one that applies 51% of the time or more. Answer all.

Description	A	Description	B
Approaches risk, decisions or change quickly	_____	Approaches risk, decisions or change slowly	_____
Frequent contributor to group conversations	_____	Infrequent contributor to group conversations	_____
Frequent use of gestures to emphasize points	_____	Infrequent use of gestures to emphasize points	_____
Often makes statements: "I'm positive"	_____	Often makes qualified statements "I think so"	_____
Emphasizes points thru confident vocal statements	_____	Emphasizes points thru explanation of information	_____
Questions tend to emphasize points	_____	Questions tend to be for clarification or support	_____
Less Patient; competitive	_____	More patient and cooperative	_____
Confronting, controlling	_____	Diplomatic; collaborative	_____
Intense; assertive	_____	Understated; reserved	_____
Tends to bend or break established rules	_____	Tends to follow established rules	_____
More challenging	_____	More accepting	_____
More talkative	_____	More quiet	_____

Total_____
(A Number Between 0-12)

Total the check marks in Column A and put the score on the Total line. Then circle the Total number on the Horizontal line on the graph on page 37.

Description	C	Description	D
Shows & Shares feelings freely	_____	Keeps feelings private	_____
Makes most decisions based on feelings (subjective)	_____	Makes most decisions based on facts (objective)	_____
Conversation includes digressions	_____	Focuses conversation on issues /tasks	_____
More relaxed and warm	_____	More formal and proper	_____
Goes with the flow	_____	Goes with the agenda	_____
Opinion oriented	_____	Fact-oriented	_____
Easy to get to know in business situations	_____	Takes time to get to know in business situations	_____
Flexible about how their time is used by others	_____	Disciplined about how their time is used by others	_____
Prefers to work with others	_____	Prefers to work independently	_____
Shows more enthusiasm than most	_____	Shows less enthusiasm than most	_____
Responsive to dreams, visions & concepts	_____	Responsive to realities, actual experiences & facts	_____
More people-oriented	_____	More task-oriented	_____

Total _____
(A Number Between 0-12)

Total the check marks in column D and put that score on the Total line. Then circle the Total number on the Vertical line in the graph on page 37.

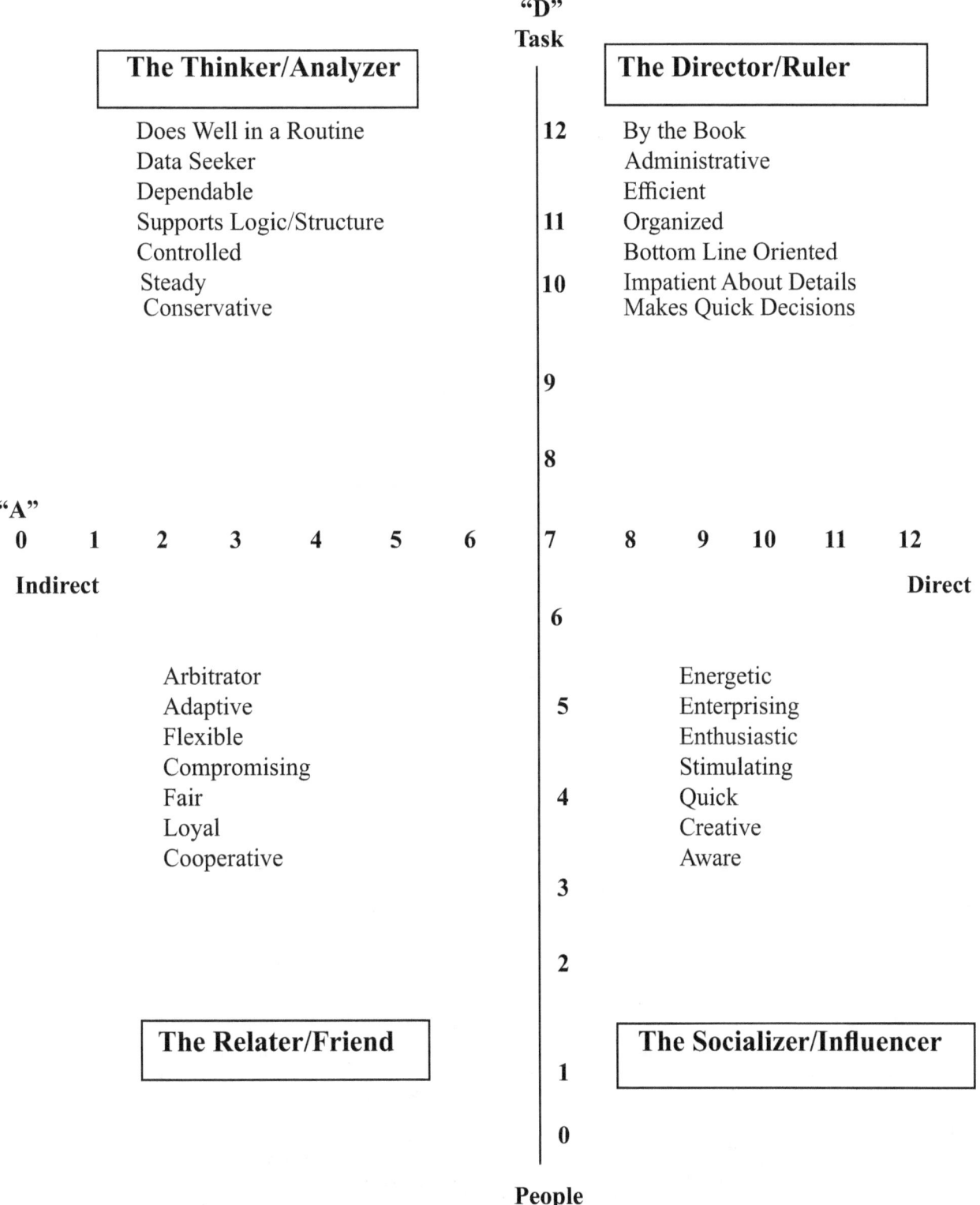

"D"
Task

The Thinker/Analyzer

12   Does Well in a Routine
Data Seeker
Dependable
11   Supports Logic/Structure
Controlled
10   Steady
Conservative

The Director/Ruler

12   By the Book
Administrative
Efficient
11   Organized
Bottom Line Oriented
10   Impatient About Details
Makes Quick Decisions

9

8

"A"

| 0 | 1 | 2 | 3 | 4 | 5 | 6 | 7 | 8 | 9 | 10 | 11 | 12 |

Indirect   **Direct**

6

Arbitrator
Adaptive
5   Flexible
Compromising
Fair
4   Loyal
Cooperative

Energetic
Enterprising
5   Enthusiastic
Stimulating
4   Quick
Creative
Aware

3

2

The Relater/Friend

The Socializer/Influencer

1

0

People

	RELATER	THINKER	DIRECTOR	SOCIALIZER
BEHAVIOR PATTERN	Open/Indirect	Self-Contained/ Indirect	Self-Contained/ Direct	Open/Direct
APPEARANCE	• Casual • Conforming	• Formal • Conservative	• Businesslike • Functional	• Fashionable • Stylish
WORK-SPACE	• Personal • Relaxed • Friendly • Informal	• Structured • Organized • Functional • Formal	• Busy • Formal • Efficient • Structured	• Stimulating • Personal • Cluttered • Friendly
PACE	Slow/Easy	Slow/Systematic	Fast/Decisive	Fast/Spontaneous
PRIORITY	Maintaining relationships	The task: the process	The task: the results	Relationships Interacting
FEARS	Confrontation	Embarrassment	Loss of control	Loss of prestige
UNDER TENSION WILL	Submit/Acquiesce	Withdraw/Avoid	Dictate/Assert	Attack/Be sarcastic
SEEKS	Attention	Accuracy	Productivity	Recognition
NEEDS TO KNOW (BENEFITS)	• How it will affect his or her personal circumstances	• How to justify the purchase logically • How it works	• What it does • By when • What it costs	• How it enhances his or her status • Who else uses it
GAINS SECURITY BY	Close relationships	Preparation	Control	Flexibility
WANTS TO MAINTAIN	Relationships	Credibility	Success	Status
SUPPORT HIS OR HER	Feelings	Thoughts	Goals	Ideas
ACHIEVES ACCEPTANCE BY	• Conformity • Loyalty	• Correctness • Thoroughness	• Leadership • Competition	• Playfulness • Being Entertaining
LIKES YOU TO BE	Pleasant	Precise	To the point	Stimulating
WANTS TO BE	Liked	Correct	In Charge	Admired
IRRITATED BY	• Insensitivity • Impatience	• Surprises • Unpredictability	• Inefficiency • Indecision	• Inflexibility • Routine
MEASURES PERSONAL WORTH BY	• Compatiblility with others • Depth of relationships	• Precision • Accuracy • Activity	• Results • Track record • Measurable progress	• Acknowledgment • Recognition • Applause • Compliments
DECISIONS ARE	Considered	Deliberate	Definite	Spontaneous

The underlying needs for each of the four personality types are quite basic:

The **Director's** need is to get the job done
The **Socializer/Influencer** wants to be noticed
The **Thinker** is concerned about accuracy
The **Relater** wants to maintain good relationships.

In order to relate to those underlying needs, you need to **develop behavioral flexibility**-"*the ability to adapt your own behavior appropriately to meet the needs of the person you are dealing with*"

If you hear **Director** behavior in a person, the first thing you want to do is to get to the point and show them what the options are. Put the decision in the Director's hands.

When you are communicating with a **Thinker,** be prepared to walk through each step. Focus on accuracy and don't rush into your conclusion. The Thinker wants to fully understand each detail along the way. Stick to your agenda, be logical, precise, and accurate.

In dealing with a **Relater,** they are very easy going. However, they are cautious about making quick decisions. Focus on developing a relationship. This personality type needs to feel comfortable with you before anything can happen. The Relater needs to be able to trust you. Take your time, put him or her at ease, and answer all questions fully.

Caution: Every personality includes Relater, Thinker, Socializer/Influencer, and Director traits.

The Bottom Line: **Learn to treat people the way they want to be treated**.

When you modify your behavior and allow that person to remain in his or her own comfort zone, tension will be reduced.

When tension goes down, cooperation goes up. When cooperation goes up... so do **YOUR SALES!!**

The choices we make in life give people clues about our personality.

What about the type of job Directors seek? A Director is strong, forceful, outgoing, competitive, and needs to be in control. They choose jobs that let them be in control. Managers, physicians, sales managers, drill sergeants; no matter what they are doing, they will run the job like a command post.

What type of job would the Thinker seek? Anything that has to do with the technical aspect of a particular field. Research, accounting, computers, and science. Thinkers are the technicians of the world.

What type of job is the Relater drawn toward? The helping professions- personnel, education, medicine, counseling, psychology, human resource development, and religious vocations.

What type of job is the Influencer/Socializer drawn to? They choose public relations, performing arts, selling, advertising, and professional speaking. In other words, anything that puts them in the spotlight. They need to be where the action is.

In summary, when you make a sales call to someone, he or she will relate to you in a very predictable pattern consistent with their personality type.

The more you can tune into a potential buyer's way of thinking and making choices, the more likely you will be able to generate sales!!

Every personality includes Director, Thinker, Relater and Socializer/Influencer traits. The behavior you see at any given time, tells you what the person's needs are at that moment.

Selling Customers
The Way They Want to Be Sold

> **People will teach you how to sell to them ...**
> **If you will pay attention to the messages they send you.**

Management and control of the tension level is one of the most effective things a seller can do to increase the likelihood of a sale. Remember, when tension is up, trust and cooperation are down. But when tension is down, trust and cooperation rise.

An extremely effective way of reducing tension is to adjust your way of communicating to accommodate the buyer's way of communicating. To do this, you learn to "read" other people and sell them in a way that they prefer to be sold. In fact, people will teach you how to sell them if you pay attention to their verbal, vocal, and body communication. Selling sometimes does not involve face-to-face communication and additional effort has to be taken in order to better understand the verbal and vocal messages.

Consultative Selling Strategies are based on building long-term relationships with clients. With this in mind, we need to know how to make relationships work for us. This focus on relationships increases our awareness of how to deal with different people in different ways. When you talk with a potential buyer, you want to know what you can do to put that buyer at ease, reduce the tension level, and open communication so that you can sell your products and services and be of assistance to that customer.

Direct & Indirect Behavior

One way to recognize the best strategy is by observing the level of directness in a person's behavior. There is a marked difference between direct and indirect behavior. On a scale from direct to indirect, very **direct** people seek to control circumstances, information, or other people by taking charge. They step right in and initiate action. **Indirect** people prefer a slower, easier going pace. They are often a little more tactful and will consider their actions carefully.

Direct people tend to be rather blunt and to the point. Indirect people ask you if you'd "like" to do something rather than tell you "what" to do. Direct people are often risk takers because they like to get on with their lives and their business. They like forward motion. Indirect people prefer to avoid risk, so they will take the least risky way of approaching a situation.

People & Task Behavior

Another behavior to observe is <u>openness.</u> Openness is a person's willingness to show what's going on inside. Open people are very relationship and **people** oriented. In a sales situation, the open person will be asking questions and making statements that focus on the two of you and the relationship you are building.

The opposite of open is <u>self-contained</u>. The self-contained person is more **task** oriented and in a sales situation, asks mostly questions that deal with the subject at hand, wanting to deal with business first and get to know you later.

Open people are more flamboyant and outgoing. They draw attention to themselves. Self-Contained people tend not to draw attention to themselves.

The Four Basic Behavioral Styles

When you combine directness and openness behaviors on a grid, the four quadrants represent the four basic behavioral styles. This combination creates four basic patterns or styles of behavior: The Director(ruler), The Thinker(analyzer), The Relater(friend), and The Socializer(influencer).

The Director (Direct and Task Oriented)

<u>Directors</u> are self-contained, meaning task oriented, direct, and fast moving. They don't mind taking a bit of risk because they want forward motion. They want progress and achievements more than anything else. These people like to run things, they want to make their own decisions.

STRENGTHS
The strengths of a **Director** are directness and ability to get the job done quickly. The Director is blunt and quite assertive and therefore gets fast results. Directors can generalize from details rather fast and see the big picture and the bottom line.

WEAKNESSES
The weaknesses of the **Director** grow out of the strengths. In that they can appear abrasive, insensitive to other people, and not concerned about details.

The Director (Direct and Task Oriented) Continued

GENERAL STRATEGIES
•Support their goals and objectives
•Keep your relationship businesslike.
•If you disagree, argue facts, not personal feelings.
•Give recognition to ideas-not the person
•To influence decisions, provide alternate actions and probabilities of their success.
•Be precise, efficient, time disciplined and well organized   .

WHEN SELLING TO THEM
PLAN to be prepared and organized, fast paced, and to the point.

MEET them in such a way that you get to the point quickly, keeping things professional and business like.

STUDY their goals and objectives, what they want to accomplish, what is happening now, and how they would like to see it changed.

PROPOSE solutions with clearly defined consequences and rewards that relate specifically to the Director's goals.

CONFIRM by providing two to three options, and let them make the decision.

ASSURE them that their time will not be wasted.

Selling Strategy: When you are selling to <u>Directors,</u> they don't want you to say, "Here's what you should do." They want you to say, "Here are your options. What do you think?" Remember, they need to make the decisions. Same outcome, different process.

Goal: Be prepared to focus on "The Results."

The Thinker (Indirect and Task Oriented)

Thinkers are indirect people. Like Relaters, they tend to move at a slow pace. Thinkers are self-contained; they focus first on the task.

STRENGTHS

Thinkers tend to be precise, efficient, and well-organized. They are task-oriented and will persevere on what might otherwise be considered a boring task.

WEAKNESSES

Their weaknesses come from an extension of their strengths, in that they are often seen as too task oriented and too cool and impersonal. They are suspected of not being concerned about feelings because they place so much emphasis on facts. They may be perceived to be nit pickers who are such perfectionists, that they can't be effective.

GENERAL STRATEGIES
•Support their organized, thoughtful approach.
•Demonstrate through actions rather than words.
•Be systematic, exact, organized, and prepared.
•List advantages and disadvantages of any plan you propose.
•Give them time to verify your words and actions.
•Follow up your personal contacts with a letter.
•Provide solid, tangible, factual evidence that what you say is true and accurate.
•Do not rush the decision-making process.

WHEN SELLING TO THEM
PLAN to be well prepared and equipped to answer all their questions.

MEET them cordially but get quickly to the task.

STUDY the situation in a practical, logical manner. Ask lots of questions and make sure your questions show a clear direction. The better your questions fit into the overall scheme of things, the more likely they are to give you the appropriate answers.

The Thinker (Indirect and Task Oriented) Continued
WHEN SELLING TO THEM

PROPOSE logical solutions to their problems. Document the how and the why, and show how your proposition is the logical thing to do.

CONFIRM as a matter of course. Don't push; give them time to think. Offer documentation.

ASSURE them through adequate service and follow-through. Be complete.

Selling Strategies: When you are selling to a <u>Thinker</u>, you want to go slowly and focus on the business at hand. Cover the details, document your claims, go through each of the steps along the way. <u>Don't skip over anything.</u>

When you approach a Thinker, start by giving him or her an outline of what you are going to do. Explain your agenda, and then stick with it!! If you get off the agenda, the Thinker will notice.

Goal: Be prepared to justify the purchase logically.

The Relater (Indirect and People Oriented)

<u>Indirect and Open</u> people are <u>Relaters</u>(friends).

Relaters like to maintain the status quo in their lives. They like their world just the way it is and are somewhat reluctant to make changes. If you propose a plan that requires major changes, they are likely to ask you to reconsider, or at least suggest a change that is not as radical.

STRENGTHS
The strengths of the Relater are warmth and the ability to build meaningful relationships with others. They are loyal and compliant. They are excellent team workers, willing to conform.

WEAKNESSES
Their weaknesses grow out of an extension of their strengths in that some people see them as too concerned about relationships to do an adequate job...

The Relater (Indirect and People Oriented) Continued

of completing the task. Directors perceive them to be slow and ineffective. They are often so sensitive to the feelings and needs of others that they are unduly influenced by them.

GENERAL STRATEGIES

- Support their feelings
- Show personal interest
- When you disagree, discuss personal opinions and feelings
- Move along in an informal slow manner
- Show that you are "actively" listening
- Provide guarantees that any actions will involve a minimum of risk
- Offer personal assurances that you will stand behind any decisions.

WHEN SELLING TO THEM

PLAN to get to know them personally. Be likable and nonthreatening, professional friendly.

MEET them by developing trust, friendship, and credibility. Go at a slow pace.

STUDY their feelings and emotional needs as well as their technical and business needs. Take time to get them to spell out what is really important to them.

PROPOSE by getting them involved. Show the human side of your proposal. Show how it affects them and their relationships with others.

CONFIRM without pushing or rushing them. Provide personal assurances and guarantees wherever you can.

ASSURE by being consistent and regular in your communication.

Selling Strategy: When you are selling to a <u>Relater</u>, recognize that major changes represent a <u>threat</u> to their established world and your plan is going to generate tension.

Goal: Be ready to reassure the Relater that everything is under control.

The Socializer/Infuencer (Direct and People Oriented)

<u>**Socializers/Influencers**</u> are direct. They move quickly, they are open, and they focus on the relationship. They are playful and spontaneous. No matter what the situation, they've got a one-liner to slip in somewhere. Socializers love variety, they hate routine. They can't stand to follow the same schedule everyday-**it drives them wild.**

STRENGTHS

The strength of a Socializer lies in his or her enthusiasm and exciting playful nature. Socializers quickly win people over and get others caught up in their drive to accomplish a task. They are fun to be with and can adapt easily to a changing situation.

WEAKNESSES

The Socializer's weaknesses result from an extension of their strengths. They sometimes come on too strong and are seen as being artificial or "put on." Some times their playfulness and spontaneity is regarded as a lack of seriousness or as impracticability. They are not good detail people in that they are easily bored by anything that tends to be monotonous or has to be done alone.

GENERAL STRATEGIES
  •Support opinions, ideas, and dreams
  •Don't hurry the discussion
  •Try not to argue
  •Agree on the specifics of any agreement.
  •Summarize in writing what you both agreed upon.
  •Be entertaining and fast moving.
  •Use testimonials to positively affect decisions.

WHEN SELLING TO THEM

   PLAN to be stimulating and interested in them. Allow them time to talk.

   MEET them boldly; don't be shy. Introduce yourself first. Bring up new topics openly.

The Socializer (Direct and People Oriented) Continued

STUDY their dreams and goals as well as their other needs.

PROPOSE your solution with stories or illustrations that relate to them and their goals.

CONFIRM the details in writing. Be clear and direct.

ASSURE that they fully understand what they have brought and can demonstrate their ability to use it properly.

Selling Strategy: When you are selling to **Socializers**, you want to be stimulating. Spend your time showing them the highlights and giving them the big picture. Do not focus on the little details.

Goal: Be flexible, be enthusiastic and let them talk. Be ready to provide them with "visual aids."

> *Lesson: Deal with people the way __they__ want to be dealt with, not just the way __you__ want to be dealt with.*

The more we know about the four personality types, the better able we are to sell to them. As a result, we know how to approach them, how to deal with them, how to manage them, and how to be successful with them.

Chapter Five

Building Block #3: Probing and Uncovering Customer Needs

The questions that salespeople ask can be more important than anything else they say to a prospect or customer. Prospects or customers may not believe the statements that a salesperson makes, but they WILL CERTAINLY BELIEVE their own answers to the questions being considered. So with this in mind, the goal of the probing phase is to uncover "agreed upon" customer needs through the skillful use of questions.

Four Reasons to Ask Questions

1. To Clarify: This approach brings your information together to see if you are on target and in agreement with the prospect/customer.
Ex: "Let me see, Ms. Jones, if I understand correctly...."

2. To Verify: This approach allows you to check your conclusions, data, or facts to confirm an existing conclusion.
Ex: "It sounds like you are planning to make a decision this week. Is that correct?"

3. To Expand: This approach permits you to seek new information on a subject you are already discussing.
Ex: "What other ways do you use these products?"

4. To Direct: This approach provides you with the ability to: change the direction of the conversation, bring up a new subject, move the buyer into ordering; or confirm the sale.
Ex: "With that in mind, how can we begin to take action to avoid those problems next month?"

Often we are required to ask questions to get information we need. In order to make sure that you are offering the right solution for the identified problem, you need to find out

as much as possible about your prospects/customers and their needs. The easiest way is to ask questions. For probing purposes, there are two types of questions that can be used and each has a particular purpose. The two types are closed-ended and open-ended questions.

Closed-Ended Questions

Most salespeople tend to ask closed-ended questions. In that way, they get exactly the information they need. It is a popular misconception that closed-ended questions are ONLY those that can be answered with a yes or no response. Closed-ended questions, sometimes called directive or fact-finding questions, can also be answered with a state -ment of fact. What distinguishes a closed-ended question from an open-ended question is that the answer is yes or no or a simple statement of fact. Nothing more needs to be said. The yes or no or simple fact completely answers each question. Ex: "Would you agree?"

Purposes of Closed-Ended Questions
•To start a conversation   •To gain the attention of someone unwilling to talk
•To gather facts   •To change the direction of a conversation
•To clarify a point   •To check for degree of interest or understanding
•To pinpoint a specific need   •To confirm an agreement

Examples of Yes or No Closed-Ended Questions
•Would this solution meet your needs?
• _____
• _____

Examples of Fact-Finding Closed-Ended Questions
•Is your _____ (insert product/service)procurement process centralized or decentralized?
• _____
• _____

Open-Ended Questions

To put a person at ease, let him or her do the talking. Salespeople must learn to perceive of themselves as being both a problem solver and valuable appreciating resource to their prospects and customers. Asking open-ended questions is a key skill toward those goals. Such questions are more conversational than closed-ended and involve more give and take. Prospects feel a greater sense of participation and involvement when they are asked open-ended questions. <u>Open-Ended Questions are designed to obtain answers that cannot be answered with a simple yes or no.</u> For example, if you ask a prospect, "Who do you currently do business with?" The answer will be a yes/no type answer and may in fact be a competitor. If you wanted the customer to discuss the particulars of why they might be doing business with a competitor, instead ask an open-ended question such as: "What are the criteria you use for determining your sources for (insert product/service) ie:software and licensing?" (An explanation is required.)

Use *open-ended questions* when you want a customer to explain or discuss something. *Closed questions* should be used when all you need is a yes, no or simple fact. Use both types of questions to gain better control of your telephone conversations.

Purposes of Open-Ended Questions
•Allow people to feel a greater sense of participation in an interview
•Give the interview a more conversational tone
•Provide more in-depth information to help you diagnose their needs
•Gain not only facts, but opinions, attitudes, and feelings
•Help prospects clarify their thinking
•Help prospects state needs in their own words
•Give you leads for paraphrasing their statements, including needs

Examples of Open-Ended Questions
•Are there other standard or non-standard software needs I can help you with?
• _____
• _____
• _____
• _____

Using Open-Ended and Closed-Ended Questions

At the beginning of most customer calls you need to learn what the customer wants so you would use open-ended questions and some fact-finding closed-ended questions. Later, you may need to employ closed-ended questions to get the customer's agreement; to understand a service request, or just to manage the conversation and your time.

Open questions begin with the words...
How, Why, When, Who, What, and Where
(The Five W's and the H)

Closed questions begin with words like...
Did, Can, Have, Do, Is, Will, and Would

Any statement can be "closed" by following it with a question...
Will that be Okay?
Do you agree?
Do you approve?
Will that be all right?

Turning Closed-Ended Questions Into Open-Ended Questions

A closed-ended question is easily turned into an open-ended question by adding one or two important words. "What," "How," and "Could" are perfect examples.

Closed: Are you standardized on any PC software?
Open: What PC software products might you be standardized on?

Closed: Is your software procurement process centralized or decentralized?
Open: Could you describe for me your organization's software procurement process?

Closed: _____

Open: _____

1. On a scale of 1-10 (with 10 being the highest), how commited are you to improving your listening? _____

2. On average, what percentage of each business day do you spend listening?_____

3. On a scale of 1-10, (with 10 being the highest), how would you rate yourself as a listener? _____

4. On a scale of 1-10, how would you rate the best listener you know? _____

5. On a scale of 1-10, how would you rate the worst listener you know? _____

6. On a scale of 1-10, (with 10 being the highest), how would the following people (where appropriate) rate you as a listener?

Manager _____	Spouse/Lover _____
Customer _____	Child(ren) _____
Close colleague _____	Best friend _____

Approximately 45% of all time spent communicating involves listening; next comes speaking with 30%, reading with 16%, and writing with 9%.

In looking at the graphic on empathic listening which appears on the next page, we can recognize that good listening is an active integrated communication skill that demands energy and know-how. It is purposeful, powerful and productive.

On the graphic, the key elements of communication are represented by the words: **Speaking, Observing and Hearing**. However, to communicate effectively we must also engage in an internal process of: **listening** (as a result of the other person speaking), **interpreting** (translating information which we selected through observing the speaker) and **evaluating** (giving meaning to our listening of the speaker's message).

Only after this internal process has been completed, can we respond appropriately.

Four Developmental Stages of Listening

Stage #1: The first and least effective stage is to **mimic content.** This is considered a first stage skill because it at least causes you to listen to what's being said. Mimicking content is easy. You just listen to the words that come out of someone's mouth and you repeat them. You've at least showed you're paying attention to his/her words. But to understand, you want to do more.

Stage #2: The second stage of empathic listening is to **rephrase the content**. It is a little more effective, but it is still limited to the verbal communication. This time you've put his/her meaning into your own words. Now you're thinking about what he/she said, mostly with the left side, the reasoning, logical side of the brain.

Stage #3: The third stage brings your right brain into operation. You **reflect feeling.** You're using both sides of your brain to understand both sides of his/ her communication.

Stage #4: Now, what happens when you use fourth stage **empathic listening** skills is really incredible. You authentically seek to understand, as you rephrase content and reflect feeling. As he/she grows in confidence of your sincere desire to really listen and understand, the barrier between what's going on inside him/her and what's actually being communicated to you disappears. They begin to trust you with their innermost tender feelings and thoughts.

What a difference real understanding can make!

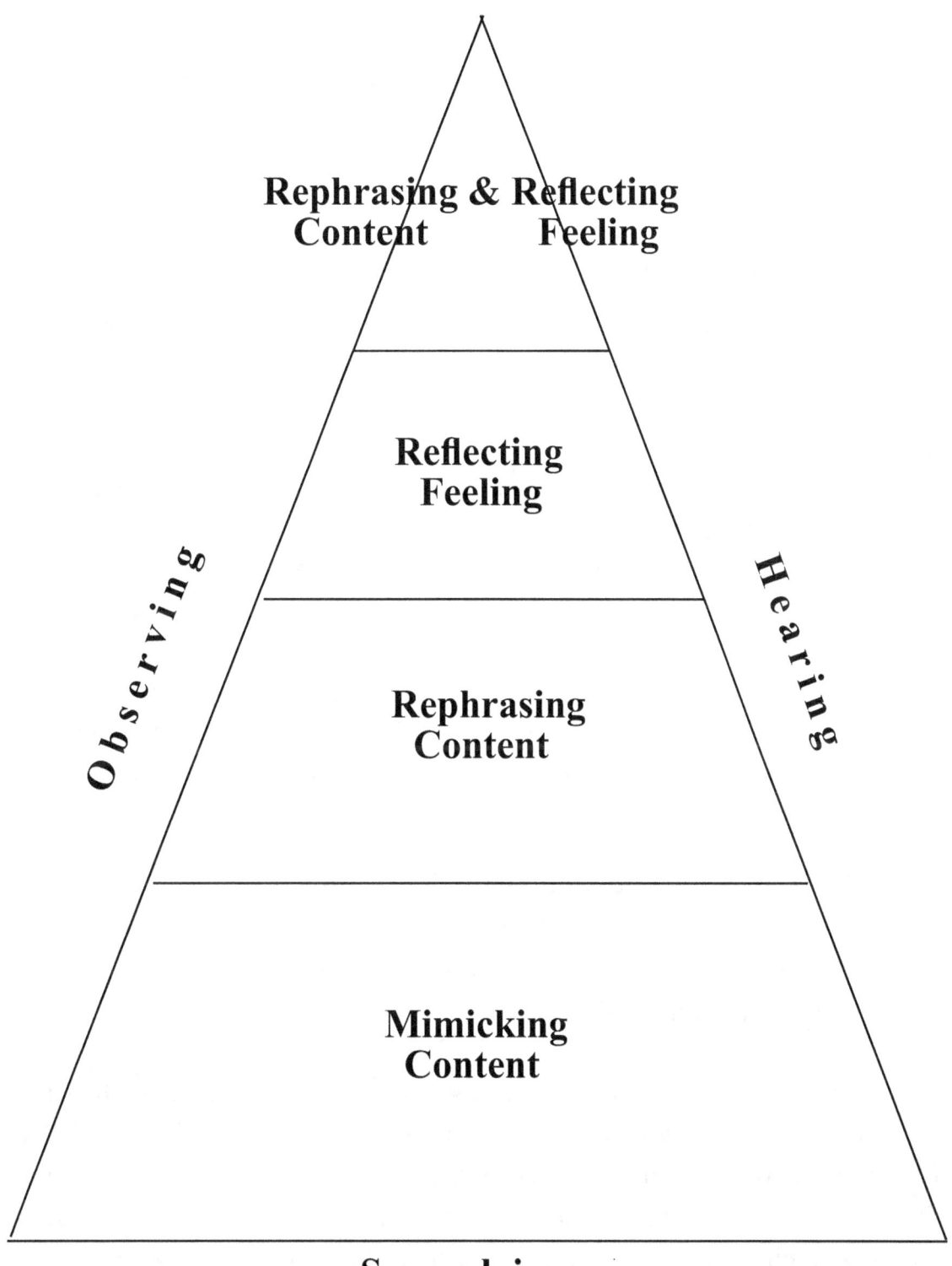

Listening for Understanding

Asking questions in sales is similar to the process used in face-to-face selling. Getting answers and listening can be trickier on the telephone, but it is a critical step to being a successful sales person. In telephone sales there are no non-verbal clues. You must create situations where you listen for feedback to steer you in the right direction.

Here are some ideas to help you actively listen for best results..
•Pause frequently.   Pause about every two sentences to invite a response.

•Vary the pace of your comments so when you do slow down, there is a space for your prospect to interrupt.

•Avoid interrupting the customer. Make sure he or she has finished a thought before you speak.

•Use silence as a tool. Allow the customer to fill the silence. Ask meaningful, open-ended questions that require more than a yes or no answer.

•Give the customer an indication that you heard what was said before returning to a sales presentation. "I hear you", "I understand, " or even simply "yes" are all useful indicators.

In a telephone conversation, you need to ask "listening" questions to see if your prospect is still with you. Examples include "How does that sound?" or "Am I making sense?" Stop immediately if the prospect interrupts you. Remember that you are in control of the conversation and will not forget where you are going.

Barriers to Effective Listening (Managing Distractions)
•Environment- Distractions about you, people, noise, traffic, smells.

•Personal - These are thoughts or problems that stem from you that block or interfere with your ability to listen to your customer.

a. Biases - Liking or disliking certain accents or areas of the country is a bias toward **regionalism** and must be avoided under all circumstances. Also, liking or disliking the discussion of specific technical questions is a bias.   In addition, allowing a previous negative telephone conversation with a particular individual to affect your current conversation with them will surely get the discussion off on the wrong footing.

b.<u>Preoccupation</u> - Thinking about what you will have for lunch, daydreaming about a vacation, wondering if you are going to have time to finish all of your calls and have all of your call time logged.

c.<u>Assumptions</u> - Jumping to conclusions about what a customer is asking or saying. Missing the customer's real problem by focusing on what you believe is the problem. Drawing on a past experience in a way that prevents you from paying attention to the current situation.

Managing Customer Distractions

a. Customer's <u>word choice</u> - becomes a distraction when the customer uses words you do not understand such as "unfamiliar technical jargon."

b. Customer's communication <u>delivery</u> is a distraction when the customer speaks abruptly, sarcastically or in a way that is difficult to understand.

Okay these Distractions Do Exist......How do I Overcome Them?
-Deep breathing - relaxes you
-Decide to listen - an act of will and determination

-Create a mental paraphrasing or brief synopsis of what the speaker just said to you. Why? Because paraphrasing helps clarify the speakers thoughts. It also prevents us from day dreaming.
-Maintain eye control, "Remember where your eyes focus, your ears will follow."

Responding with Decisiveness

We can never respond decisively if we have not developed active listening skills. We must listen to not only the words expressed but also the meaning. Selling is essentially oral communication. When you sell over the phone, you have to pay more attention to language, both yours and your prospects. Your sole vehicle is language--words and inflections. You'll learn to recognize and react decisively to the subtle signals buyers communicate with their voices. One example is, "I'm perfectly happy with my existing vendor." How would you respond with decisiveness to this statement from a customer?

What are other examples of subtle signals that buyers communicate that require a sales associate to respond with decisiveness?

- _____
- _____

Chapter Six

Building Block #4: Tailoring Your Sales Presentation

Good Presentations Begin with a Plan

It takes many hours to develop and hone a good planned presentation. But the advantages are tremendous. Such a presentation provides a way to inform and obtain information from your prospect (potential customer) without confusing her. It should be clear, concise, and easy to follow. And remember that a confused person has difficulty making a buying decision.

Instead, she hems and haws, feeling incapable of making a decision that involves money. The easiest thing for her to do is procrastinate--delay the transaction. But a good presentation is designed to make it easy for the prospect to buy. It gives her a step-by-step method by which she can share information about her organization and obtain your product or service.

Perhaps more than anything else, **a planned presentation gives you direction.** The idea is to begin with the end in mind...closing the sale. And with a well thought out presentation, the exact route to your destination has been carefully considered and mapped out. Without this map, you can be easily sidetracked by objections and lose your sense of purpose. With it, everything you say helps get you to the destination; each sales point complements the others.

Elements of Your Sales Presentation

In a telephone sales presentation, you always have the advantage over the individual you are calling, because you can be prepared in advance. **You are the expert.**

You have more knowledge about your product and company, and about the competition, then she does—**if you do your homework as a professional**. Keep in mind that a sales presentation applies to **both** your Inbound Sales and Outbound Sales calls with customers and prospects.

As you prepare your presentation, keep in mind the following six factors:

•Knowing Your Product and Service: You must know and tell what your products and services are and how they can satisfy the needs of your customers. Your product information is extremely important as it serves as the heart of your presentation. However, you aren't paid to pass on information. You're paid to produce sales. So, while the product story is vital, you should design your presentation to create **the desire for action**. Remember: "It's great to tell—but you are paid to sell."

•Knowing Your Philosophy and Purpose: The basic element of every good presentation is a philosophy or purpose. A universal characteristic of great salespeople is that they do not perceive themselves as people who simply purvey a product such as insurance, stocks or computer equipment. **They see themselves as <u>professionals who offer something unique</u> to their customers.** These professionals have a basic philosophy and purpose that they believe can meet the needs of the prospect. They have a potential way of **adding-value** or **creating personal satisfaction.** The product or service they sell is simply the practical vehicle that attains the results.

"Solution Sales" is the only option to compete in today's highly competitive technology industry. As a result, sales professionals are listening and selling "solutions" to their customers effectively. The order takers are not. Your philosophy and purpose must be to address customer's needs by providing them with the solutions they desire to meet with success.

By adhering to this philosophy and striving to achieve the above purpose, you will **yourself be sold**. Thereby freeing yourself from the limiting bonds of "selling for selling's sake" and giving you the ability to not simply "sell" but to feel as though you are serving the greater good of the business community.

•Are You Sold Yourself: Every field is dominated by nonprofessionals who have no personal commitment to themselves, their customers or their company. They limit themselves to selling a specific product instead of using the product or service as a means for the prospect to attain broader objectives. Sales professionals who offer **solutions** which are designed to solve business needs include the elements of conviction and urgency into their presentation. Conviction addresses the fact that you are the best person to satisfy your prospect's needs. And your sense of urgency, creates a framework that allows your prospect to see that it is in his advantage to act—now!

•**Understanding Your Prospect's Needs:** Another key ingredient in a good presentation is personal two-way communication. Through effective communication, you gain a personal understanding of the prospect's needs. What are your prospect's plans for the next six months? How can the two of you work together to ensure her success? If she considers you her friend, as well as a conscientious and knowledgeable person, your working relationship with her will become a lifetime one. So get to know your prospect on a personal basis.

•**The Most Important Part of the Presentation is to "Add-Value":** A presentation has an introduction, body and a close. The average busy person begins to get impatient after five minutes on the telephone, and sometimes sooner. This structure allows you to get **immediately** to the heart of the presentation—**differentiating yourself and your organization** in the mind of your prospect. In three or four minutes, you have introduced yourself and the company, as well as "added-value" by asking your prospect strategic questions which will assist you in making her a "customized offer."

•**Practice, Practice, Practice:** Whether or not you memorize your presentation, you will need to practice it. As the old adage goes, "It's not what you say, but how you say it that is important." Nowhere is this truer than in sales. The best presentation will fail if it sounds canned. And it will sound canned, whether you read it or memorize it, unless you practice, practice, practice.

Tailoring Your Sales Presentation

Whether you're handling an inbound or outbound sales call, it's important to remember a few key points when establishing rapport with your customers. Just as each of us are at different levels of sales and technical skill, so are our customers. As each Account Executive has their own unique style, so does each customer. Let your customer set the pace and style for the phone call. Remember, your job is to provide solutions, so LISTEN to what the customer is telling you, and TAILOR your communication to their needs.

After you have executed your plan, established yourself with the right person and asked your probing questions, what happens next? It's now time for your presentation. During this time, you should be able to uncover one or more potential needs for your products and services. How do you put this information in the most attractive format? To maximize the power of your presentation, concentrate on the following five areas:

#1. Gain Your Customer's Agreement
Prospect Checklist...
•Do you have enough information about the prospect and organization?
•Does the prospect have a probable need that you can fill?
•Does the prospect have the ability to buy?
•Does the prospect have the authority to make the buying decision?

•Does the prospect have enough awareness of your company to understand and appreciate what you have to offer?

> You need to obtain the answers to the above questions and communicate the "Value-Added" advantages of doing business with you and your organization prior to making your presentation to the prospect.

Once you have completed the above, you have now determined that your customer is no longer a **suspect** (someone who may use your product or services), but is a genuine **prospect** (does use your product or services or one's similar to yours). So, therefore, it is now worth your time to continue to establish a relationship with her in order to offer solutions to her needs.

•**Summarize the important points** of your fact-finding with your customer. Even though you think you have heard everything correctly, you may be mistaken on a critical point.

•**Get your customer agreeing with you.** This is the other benefit of summarizing the information you uncovered in probing. As you relate accurate information back to your customer, her reaction is to agree. This also "softens her up," and gets her in the habit of saying yes, or agreeing with you. An excellent technique for accomplishing this is to start with a confirming question—- **"Do you agree that.....?" (Closed Question Alert!)**

•**Listen for your customer's "hot buttons."** If you have done a good job of probing (and you need to in order to make a strong presentation), you have probably discovered several needs your customer has that you can satisfy. However, some of these needs are more important than others.

•**Ask customers to list their needs according to importance.** You may think you know what's important, but you could be totally wrong. You not only can get customers to tell you what they think is important, but you also can get them involved in working toward a solution.

#2. Use Benefits

You have now identified the problem, challenge or issue that is most important to your customers, and you have them agreeing with you. Now is the time to present your solution to their problem or need.

To maximize your effectiveness and be most persuasive, **you need to explain your solution in terms of how it will help or benefit them or their business** . Never forget the difference between **features** (characteristics or facts) of a product/service and the **benefits** (the value received)...WIIFM: What's in it for me as the customer?, What is the advantage to me as the customer? and What can it do for the customer?). Remember, the benefits are what sell the product/service. Make sure you can compare your product/services to the competition if asked. This requires you to have an excellent knowledge of both the product/service you are selling and the competition.

> The Winning Presentation Formula: **Need + Product + Benefit = Solution**

#3. Justify the Cost

Your customer now believes in you and you have shown her how using your product/service will address her need. Finished? Not yet. You need to help your customer build a business case for buying your product/service. The best way to do this is to cost justify, or show how the dollar amount of the benefits will exceed the cost of purchasing the product/service.

To make the process of cost justifying easier, there are certain steps you can take:

•Determine what aspect of your customer's problem, challenge or issue, you are helping. What savings of time, money or resources are you providing?

•Clarify exactly how you are going to help your customers with these issues. Will you help increase their sales? Will you decrease their costs? Make sure your solution fits your customers' plan and doesn't cost more than it makes.

•Translate the projected increase or decrease into dollars.

•Finally, compare the benefits your customer will enjoy to the cost of your solution.

Role-Play Scenario: Let's use this technique in a customer/Account Executive scenario or role play activity. Here are three details for the Account Executive to keep in mind when they are speaking with a prospect/customer.

1. Identify and confirm your prospect or customer's needs.
2. Get a qualified picture of their current situation.
3. Show them the benefits of your solution, including the profit potential or savings as a result of your product/service.

It takes practice, but after you have used this technique a few times, you'll be able to quickly identify the hot issues and key benefits that will make your presentations more effective.

Tailoring Your Sales Presentation Roundtable Discussion Topics:

A. How do we add impact to our sales presentations using the following:
- •⟩ Analogies
- •⟩ Humor
- •⟩ Drama
- •⟩ Pauses and Silence
- •⟩ Visualization

B. Give an example of how you can tailor a presentation to a customer based on the benefits and advantages of any specific product. Do you have a success story to share on this topic?

C. How can a non-technical sales professional provide technical solutions to our customers? Can we divulge the fact that we are not computer software and hardware technicians, without losing the customer's confidence?

D. What kinds of probing questions can we ask to find solutions to customer needs?

E. How do we use our resources to help provide the solutions?

Chapter Seven

Building Block #5: Handling Prospect Questions/Objections

Welcome Customer Objections

An **objection** is a reason given by prospects when they are not ready to buy your product or service. Many sales people fear objections, because these objections get in the way of a sale. **But the most difficult objection to deal with is the one you don't hear.** For example, a sales pro fears **not hearing objections**, because chances are the prospects have objections, but they are just not bothering to tell him. And if he doesn't know about the objections in their heads, then he will never get the opportunity to address and overcome them.

The sales pro also doesn't interpret an objection as a rejection, whereas many novice sales people do. To the sales pro, an objection does not mean no, but rather, **"I'm not convinced yet.** Give me a more compelling reason to buy this product or service from you and your organization."** This sales pro doesn't react negatively to the objection, but instead, welcomes the objection as an opportunity to address the prospects questions and objections.

Three Reasons to Welcome Customer Objections

Objections may not always be easy to manage, but they provide the sales professional with positive feedback because:

1.) Objections communicate that the BUYER is ENGAGED in the conversation.

2.) You can take advantage of the opportunity to demonstrate how YOU, YOUR PRODUCT/SERVICE, and/or YOUR COMPANY can ADD VALUE.

3.) They SIGNAL that the BUYER is qualified and qualified buyers have the means to purchase your goods and services.

Listening for Content: There are essentially three types of expressions you hear from customers. Customers will:

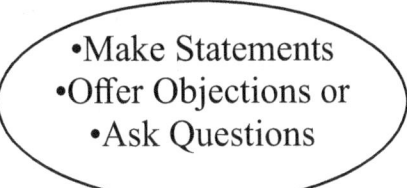

•Make Statements
•Offer Objections or
•Ask Questions

Also, there are three things that can happen when you fail to listen closely.

1. You will hear what you want to hear.
2. You will hear what you expect to hear.
3. You will not recognize the difference between a statement, objection or question.

Managing Objections: An objection occurs when the customer is opposed to the proposed plan of action. When you hear an objection it is important to address it immediately. If the customer offers an objection and you ignore it, you may have lost a customer.

If you ignore objections or questions, a customer will usually:
1. Stop you and repeat the objection or the question
2. Not say anything to you but still be dissatisfied because you ignored them, and walk away.

Summary: Managing Objections

1. Listen to what the caller says.
2. Always provide an immediate response.
3. State the response in clear and positive terms.
4. Do not provide unnecessary information and conversation.

> **Customers will let you know when they object to something and their objections will usually be direct and to the point. Your job is to listen and respond appropriately.**

Read the following expression as if it were delivered to you on the telephone. Then indicate with an S , if you think it is a (statement), a Q if you think it is a (question) or a O for those items that you believe are an (objection). Assume that all responses have been made in a normal tone of voice. (All punctuation has purposely been left out.)

1. _____ I think your service is quite good.

2. _____ Your turn around time for delivery is too long.

3. _____ Why does the bill show $107.00.

4. _____ Your prices are higher than my current supplier.

5. _____ You don't understand. I need some technical help now.

6. _____ When will it be in stock.

7. _____ What are you going to do about the _____.

8. _____ I can't wait. I need to talk with her today.

9. _____ Why is he never available when I need him.

10. _____ I am not going to pay this bill.

Answers: See bottom of page 91 for
          Answer Key

Why Does a Prospect Object?

In the great majority of cases, <u>an objection is not a refusal but rather a request for additional information</u>. The sale does not terminate when an objection is voiced. On the contrary, this is where real selling begins because a challenge has been presented which must be addressed by the sales person. True sales pros know that <u>most of their sales are closed after the prospect has expressed objections</u> so what they do as a result of responding to these customer objections will determine whether the interaction culminates in a sale.

Let's look at several common reasons why prospects object:

•**Request for Information:** The customer may just need some information clarified or may not have enough information because the sales person lacked the appropriate responses or was unable to successfully communicate the *features and benefits* of the solution.

•**Price Objections:** This could be a stall tactic or a question of whether the prospect perceives that the product's value outweighs the cost. In addition, the prospect might have other questions/objections on his mind such as: "How does this product/service and it's price compare with the competition?" or "Am I getting the best deal (or value) for my money?"

•**Personal Objections:** The person may have a bias toward you for no legitimate reason or may distrust sales people in general because of something in the past. Signs of this can be silence, sarcasm or open hostility.

•**Approval:** The prospect may have been delegated the task to research the purchase and make recommendations to a superior. Therefore, he may have a legitimate issue such as:

-needing approval,
-needing to obtain a purchase order number prior to purchase,
-not authorized to exceed a specific budgeted dollar amount,
-needing to have multiple quotations/bids or
-not wanting to wait on backorder status.

Understanding Price Objections

Price objections are the most common and the toughest objections to deal with. The customers and territories you deal with are all competitive and demanding. Add the fact that most of your buyers are experienced, and you have a very risky situation to neutralize. Your ability to answer this objection in a positive style can be the difference between closing the sale or losing the sale.

Questions to ask Yourself in Dealing with Price Objections:

•Is price really your prospect's main objection?
•How badly does your prospect need your product?
•How serious is his resistance to price?
•Is your prospect telling you the truth?
•Is your prospect trying to get a "low ball" price to bargain with your competition?

•If your prospect is comparing your price against a competitive price, is your prospect comparing exact products/services and their features/benefits, including whether items are in stock and deliverable within ___hours or ___days?
•Will your prospect buy if the price is right?

Guidelines to use in Dealing with Price Objections:

•**Set Your Customers' Expectations By Not Getting a Reputation for Being "Easy".**
You need your customers' respect to keep their loyalty. Cutting your price can lead to the feeling that you don't have confidence in yourself or your products or services and their ability to stand on their own merit. **This can lead to setting a customer expectation that "everything is negotiable" and it will become a dangerous spiral of customers always anticipating price adjusting.** Be proud of your value as a "sales consultant" and not an order taker. Also be proud of the products and services and excellent customer service standards of your company.

•Make Yourself an Added-Value in the Mind of Your Customers. Distinguish yourself from your competition by doing extra things for your customers—things that a lower price can't compensate for. Treat their business like your own. Become a valuable appreciating resource to your customers by looking out for their best interests. Call them and suggest ideas to reduce costs or make their job easier or more productive. These are advantages that lower prices can't compare against.

•Know Your Buyers and Their Needs. The more you know about your prospects and their needs, the more you can personalize your approach to handle their price objections.

•Anticipate Price Resistance. Keep track of the common objections (and even some of the uncommon ones). You may want to break them down by customer or industry profile. This preparation pays off.

•Talk Savings. If your product or service is priced higher than the competition, speak in terms of the value added features of you and your company.

•Approach Your Prospects Practical and Realistic Side. You get what you pay for. Customers who buy a product at a ridiculously low price know that something isn't right. They'll get less service or poor technical or warranty support later.

•Make Sure Your Customers Know the Risk They Are Taking. If they are an existing customer, make sure they realize they're sailing into uncharted waters if they end up doing business with a competitor <u>simply based on price. They know what they'll get from you.</u> The new company may not guarantee what you can.

•Convince Your Prospects That You Offer a Better Value. Don't bad-mouth your competition—just sell the quality and benefits of your products and services. The more benefits you discuss, the easier it becomes for your customers to draw their own conclusions, hopefully positive, about you and your company's products and services.

Understanding Procrastination Objections

Another common objection is **procrastination** and to deal with this objection effectively, you need to **determine what motivates your prospect**.

Prospect Motivations.

•**Recognition.** About 50% of prospects fit into this category. They want approval from others. The strategy for dealing with these people should be to stress the company and product prestige.

•**Security.** About 25% of your prospects need security. They don't like risks. They have to believe that your product or service will provide them with a risk-free experience. To deal with this type of buyer, be sure to stress dependability and limited risks.

•**Achievement.** The last 25% of your buyers fit into this category. These buyers are look - ing for gain. To appeal to them, concentrate on increased performance with your products or services or enhanced productivity or savings of *time or money*.

Your key strategy in determining what motivates your prospect is to determine if they have **a desire for achieving reward or a desire to avoid pain**. By determining which desire has priority, you can appeal to their stronger motivation and seriously reduce the chance of procrastination. To accomplish this, you have **to listen very carefully** to what your prospects' emphasize.

Here are some hints on how to appeal to each of these motivational needs:

Recognition Needers.

•Relate a successful sales story of another customer.
•Use references (customer's names, with their permission) to add credibility.
•Be ready with other customer's opinions and experiences.

•Make sure your customer knows what you and your products and services can do that no other competitor can.

Security Needers.

•Sell the quality of your products and services and of your company. Also make sure you convince your customer of your own credibility.

•When dealing with a competitive situation, stress positive comparisons (which favor your products and services). Don't speak negatively about your competition.

Achievement Needers.

•Be open with your customers. Don't disguise issues. Face them head on.

•Speak to your customers in terms of performance. They want to know the bottom line.

•Talk price when asked. This may be a time where you need to handle those price objections from achievers.

Resisting Decision Making

Whether your prospect is motivated by the need for recognition, security or achievement isn't as important as the fact that **EVERY** prospect at one time or another **resists decision making**. Usually the reason for this is that **deciding can be risky.**

They might make the wrong decision and no one wants to make the wrong decision. However, they also realize that decisions are necessary, even during those times when they might not have enough time or information to fully explore and contemplate their actions. With this reality in mind, it's your job to convince them that by not acting they will be making a decision that can work against them. (Not making a decision, is in fact a decision!)

They are often aware of their inability to take what they know is the right action, and although they seem to resist, they may really **want your help** in making a wise purchase. As a sales professional, it is your job to show them how to make an affirmative buying decision.

> **Remember: By determining what motivates your prospects and how you can respond to their "hot buttons," your chances for sales success increase greatly.**

Strategies for Overcoming Objections

Every objection, whether minor or major, must be treated with respect and diplomacy. Sales professionals know that there is no such thing as an unworthy objection. They know that if it is important to the prospect, it sure needs to be addressed by the sales associate. They also know that **the objective is not to overcome all objections; the objective is to close the sale.**

Overcoming objections is a delicate process which must be done in such a way that the prospect feels comfortable with the removal of his objections. He must want to do business with you not only because you know your products and services but because of your sincere desire to help him. Here are some Guidelines:

-Objections should be handled tactfully but directly.
-Whatever the objection might be, take it seriously and meet it head-on.
-But be careful to empathize with the prospect and respect his way of thinking.
-The prospect should be invited into the conversation.
-Objections should never be answered in a hostile manner.

> **Your purpose is to create a transaction, not to win the conversation**

Common Objections and Techniques for Addressing Them

•**No Need:** "If I could show you how_____ could benefit you, would you consider it?" or 'What are you using now?"

•**No Hurry:** "Do you realize that by waiting you may be giving a competitive edge to your competition?" or "When would you want to get it?"

•**No Money:** (see below)

•**No Ability to Pay for It:** "We have the ability to set up a credit limit for your company if you qualify." or "Did you know that we can help you establish a line of credit." or "Who else in your organization should we be talking with?" (who may have the ability to pay for it).

Can't Afford It: "Can't afford it?" (The echo technique.) "What is it that you can afford?" or "If I could show you something within your budget, would you consider it?"

•**No Trust:** "I understand how you feel. As your Account Manager, what would I have to do to earn your trust again?" or "What can I do to regain your trust?" or "What was the issue or problem?" or "Where did we go wrong?....I will personally guarantee you that I will not permit that to happen again."

Answer the Objection and Close the Sale

Once you answer an objection, you should always ask for the order again. We will address Closing Techniques in Chapter 8, although, here is a general rule for closing more sales:

Request the Order Three Times. After each objection, present the prospect with a complete explanation—and request the order. The sales associate who asks for the order three times will be far more successful than the one who makes only one request. Studies have shown that <u>when three requests are made instead of one</u>, **productivity can increase five -fold**. Imagine that....by asking for the order three times, you increase your productivity fivefold! That is a number that can be measured in dollars and multiplying those dollars by 5 is impressive.

How To Handle Specific Objections: An Exercise

On the following page are several of the most common objections that customers raise and some specifics on how to address them. This information will be used to provide an opportunity for participants to practice responding to them. Review this listing and write down some specific ways you would address them with a prospect. Because the key to handling objections is preparation and practice, participants will discuss their techniques with the group and role-play a variety of prospect/sales associate scenarios on handling objections.

Overcoming Price Objections

•Quote the Price in Terms that Avoid "Sticker Shock." If your price sounds too high, rephrase it so it sounds less costly.

•Offer Leasing As an Alternative. If you sell an expensive product, system or service, offer leasing as a cost-effective alternative to direct purchase.

•Stress Cost of Ownership versus Cost of Purchase. The purchase price is not the only cost of owning something. There is the cost of maintenance, support, repair, refurbishment, operation, supplies, and, when something wears out, replacement. Therefore the product that costs the least to buy may not actually cost the least to own; often it is the most expensive to own.

•Create an Apples-to-Oranges Comparison. When the prospect can compare two items and find them exactly identical, the price becomes the deciding factor, and the low-priced bidder wins. Fortunately, products and services are rarely identical. Multiple differences, some major, some minor, make it virtually impossible to price-compare a large percentage of goods and services with an apples-to-apples comparison. As soon as doing such a comparison is made impossible, you can counteract price objections by pointing out the differences (advantages) of your offer compared to the competition's.

•Scale It Back. Many people want to buy things they cannot afford. When your initial offer is too rich for the prospect, scale it back. Prospects with limited funds—and that's almost everyone —understand that they can't have everything they want or the top-of-the-line model with all the accessories all the time.

•Use a Differentiator. A **differentiator** is a quality or feature that differentiates you, your products and services from the competitions. The key is to make the prospects understand that, although two products may be virtually identical, no two are supported by the supplier in exactly the same way. It is the differences between the way you render after-sale support and services versus the competitor's operation that enables you to say to prospects, "The slightly higher prices we charge are a drop in the bucket compared with the quality and results you get." Of course, you must back up this claim with details and proof.

•**Target Value-Conscious Buyers.** Fortunately, a large number of prospects do not buy solely on price. Most of them instead want to make sure they are getting **the most value for their money**. They are willing to pay a higher price if they feel they are getting a superior solution. Don't try to convince someone who always picks the lowest-priced product they shouldn't do so. Instead, target value buyers. Focus the conversation on demonstrating to them that you offer the best value.

•**Remind Prospects that Cheaper Is Not Always Better.** Most prospects know that you get what you pay for, and that the cheapest price is not necessarily the best price. Therefore, reminding prospects that cheaper is not better can be an effective tactic in preventing them from buying on price only or on price primarily.

•**Handling Objections that Result from Misunderstandings**

The problem may be with your presentation, your product or your company. Perhaps they don't understand a term you are using, or are irritated about not knowing their price. You'll never know unless and until you ask. Once you know what's troubling your prospect, you can clear up any misunderstanding and ask for the sale.

•**Handling Objections that Result from Time Delays**

"I want to think it over" indicates that the prospect has doubts about the product or is afraid of making a decision. The sales professional asks targeted questions and uses empathy to uncover the real reason for the hesitation.

Examples: "I see that this is a difficult decision for you. What is it that you would like to think about?" or "I understand how you feel. What are some of the reasons that speak for and against buying at this time?"

**The Key to Effectively Handling Prospect Objections is to:
Find Out What's Important to the Prospect and Address The Concern.**

Chapter Eight

Building Block #6: The A, B, C's of Closing the Sale

Gaining Customer's Commitment to Buy

OK, you have found a solution for your customer. It meets all of their specifications, and it fits their budget requirements. Now, how do we get them to buy it? The purpose of this section is to develop closing strategies. In simple terms, **closing** means getting the order and the sale is considered "closed" when the customer makes a commitment to buy. Some sales pros view a sale as "closed" only AFTER it has been shipped to the customer!!!

The most important part of your job is closing sales, but often very little time is spent in preparation of the close. There are three parts to sales;

1. getting the customer to consider your organization as a supplier,
2. selling them on the reasons for doing business with your organization, and
3. getting them to buy from you!

Always Be Closing....

Closing is necessary because it overcomes prospect resistance, inertia and uncertainty.

Prospects are <u>resistant</u> because, like most people, they hate to part with money. They suffer from <u>inertia</u>, the natural tendency of all objects, animate and inanimate, to resist action and movement. Worse, they are also, to a degree, <u>uncertain</u>, in that even if they want to buy from you, they're not quite sure what to order or how to go about it.

> **When people are unsure** what to do next, **their choice is to do nothing**.

If You Want Your Prospect's Business, You've Got to Ask For It

Many sales people think of closing as the last phase of a sales call. If you do, you may not get all the sales that you could. During every sales call there are several opportunities to close the sale so the idea to **Always Be Closing** applies throughout a call with a prospect.

How? Begin with trial closes (questions which illicit customer response and support for the purchase), such as, "Is this what you were looking for?" and "Can you imagine how this will boost your productivity?"

Obviously, these responses come after you have listened to your customer and perhaps probed them further for information on their needs. They are also in direct response to a dialogue that you have established with your prospect.

Now that you have planned your presentation through introduction, probing and objections, it's time to look at some sample closing techniques. There are three critical phases to closing:

•Using Trial Close Questions
•Identifying Buying Signals, and
•Closing Techniques

Phase I: Using Trial Close Questions
There are two types of questions used in closing.

-**Trial closes** are questions that get **OPINIONS.**
-**Closing** questions get **DECISIONS.**

When you are not sure a prospect is ready to buy, use a trial close. Trial closes give you an indication of how well you have convinced the prospect so far. You are helping prospects to clarify their thinking. Trial closes are nonthreatening. It is easier to offer an opinion than it is to make a decision. So, by asking a trial close question, the prospect can offer his opinion which allows the idea of making a decision to soak in gently.

> **Getting positive responses from trial closes indicates to you**
> **when to ask a closing question.**

Examples of Trial Close Questions

•Can you see how this _____ would meet your requirements?
•At this point, how do you feel about _____?
•Which of these do you like best?
•Is this what you had in mind?
•Is this an improvement over what you are doing now?
•What do you think of this?
•Does this make sense to you?
•In your opinion, do you feel that....?

Additional Trial Close Questions:

• _____

• _____

• _____

• _____

Phase II: Identifying Verbal Buying Signals

Most salespeople experience a normal fear of rejection and cope with it as well as can be expected. Often more difficult for salespeople to correct is their failure to recognize and act upon a client's verbal buying signals.

The best salespeople listen far more often then they talk, usually in a ratio of 70/30, listening to talking. Learning to recognize prospect buying signals can be compared to following the traffic law at a railroad crossing: STOP, LOOK & LISTEN.

Good salespeople...

> **STOP TALKING, START WATCHING and always KEEP LISTENING.**

Phase III: Watch and Listen for these and similar buying signals

When you are selling to customers over the phone, you must rely on verbal buying signals. Following are several examples of good verbal buying signals. When you hear these questions, you can be sure you have your customer's interest, and desire to purchase. They may come soon after you introduce yourself to your prospect, they may come part way through your presentation, or they may not come at all. Always be listening for them, though. Watch and listen for these and similar buying signals.

•**Silence.** Generally this will not be a buying signal if it happens too early in the call. Your prospect may be waiting for you to prove you have something worth his time. However, if you have gone through a presentation, answered several objections and hear silence on the other end of the phone line—go for the close. His silence may be telling you that you have answered all of his objections and he's ready to say yes.

•**Implementation Questions.** Questions like "How soon can it be delivered?" "What's the turnaround time to receive that _____?" and "What are your company's terms?" tell you that your customer may have made a decision to buy and is moving on to implementing that purchase.

•**Reference of Ownership.** If you hear your customer say something like, "I can use that on the project that I'm starting next month," or "I can really take care of my important account with that," try closing him. Confirm these feelings by asking for the sale. Other examples: "Can you go over the specs with me again?", "I could…(customer makes reference to what they could do with your product offering)."

• **Small Details.** When your customer starts talking about small details concerning your products or services, he may be ready to say yes. Example: " Can I get that delivered by Wednesday?"

<u>**What are some other examples of verbal buying signals?**</u>

Techniques to Confirm Agreement and Close The Sale

> • **Summarize:**
>   -Start By Summarizing Agreed-Upon Needs
>
> • **Assume the Agreement**
>   -You Assume that you have Identified Needs,
>   -You have Presented Appropriate Solutions, and
>   -Now it is Time to Get Started.
>
> • **Ask for the Commitment**
>   -Closing a sale is simply asking the customer to buy.
>   -It is a natural stage in the entire sales process.

Proven Closing Techniques

Once you have identified the signal that your customer is ready to close, you need to complete the sale. **More sales are lost by failing to ask for the sale** than for any other reason. So with this in mind, lets now focus on the actual close. There are lots of ways to ask for a sale. Lets make a list of some good closing questions. These types of questions should be part of every successful sales professional's vocabulary.

The Next Step Close Answer prospect's question and then ask for her commitment by posing an open ended question that seeks direction:
        -What do you see as our next step?
        -How should we proceed?
        -Where do we go from here?

The Direct Close....Ask for the Sale! You must ask in order to get the sale and asking three times during your conversation with a prospect enhances your ability to close.
"Would you like me to place this order for you?" (Closed Question Alert!)
"Does this make sense to you?" (Closed Question Alert!)
"Shall we go ahead with this order?" (Closed Question Alert!)
"This will help your staff be more productive, right? (Closed Question Alert!)

The "Small Decision" Close. This is where you assume the prospect has made up his mind to buy your product or service and only needs to work out some of the minor details. It takes for granted that you have already made the sale.

"Whose attention should we ship this to?"

"Where would you like this delivered?"

"Would you like two day shipping on this?"

"How soon would you like this?"

"How would you like to pay for that?"

Features and Benefits Close. Detail features (characteristics or facts of a product/service) and benefits of purchase (the value received....what is the advantage to me as the customer). Make certain that the prospect understands the reasons why this solution is the one that will work for them by telling them point by point the features and benefits of this product or service.

Now or Never Close. The objective behind this close is to give the customer a sense of urgency. This close is perfect for a backordered item, upsell or a manufacturer's promotion that is only being offered for a limited time.

"I have ____ number in stock and the price is going up as of _____."

"I offered you special pricing for this quote which will expire at the end of the month."

The Forced Choice or Alternate Choice Close. This close gives your customer a choice of products or services to purchase. The decision to buy is placed squarely in the hands of the prospect. You're just offering your products as the two choices. "Would you like to order the _____ or _____?"

"Would you like to pay for this on credit card or open account?

Safety in Numbers Close. This close appeals to one's natural instinct to want to fit in and to be a part of something that has proven itself to be effective.

"This is the most popular product of it's kind on the market today."

"They're selling so well, you want to be sure to get this while it's still in stock."

Answer Question with a Question Close. This close essentially answers the prospect's question with a question.

"When can it be delivered?, When would you like it delivered?"

"Do you have anything less expensive?, What is your budget on this project?"

"What payment terms do you accept?, What would you like to use?"

Contingency Close. This close and the sale is contingent upon the satisfaction of a certain condition.

"OK, if we can deliver this product by January 1, can you think of any reason why we should not go ahead with the order?"

Mirror Close. You want to repeat the objection back to the customer in the form of a question.

"Too Expensive?"... "Too Expensive?"

The customer said the item was too expensive. You want the customer to tell you why they think it is too expensive. Wait for them to answer your question?

Ben Franklin Close. List the pros and cons of the item the customer is interested in. You list the pros and let the customer list or think about the cons. If the buying decision is being based on the BENEFITS then there should be more reasons to buy than not to buy.

Columbo Close. You use this close when the prospect believes you are not going to make the sale today. Your objective is to get more information so you can close again.

"What else could I have done to help you make your decision?"

"Oh, I didn't realize that I didn't mention that we do have _____ available for our corporate customers. Let me explain the details to you."

Summary Close. Summarizes both the prospect's need and a solution which emphasizes the benefits of the purchase.

"Let's just briefly go over what we've discussed." Let's summarize....You said you needed...

Guarantee Close. This close informs the prospect that the item may be returned within 30 days for any reason. This close should only be used as a last resort and **ONLY** on Money Back Guarantee (MBG) products.

"The product does come with a 30 day money back guarantee. May I place the order for you?"

Closing Summary

Remember, on every call in which you plan to close a sale, be ready with your closing questions. No close works 100% of the time. Likewise, not every prospect gives you clear buying signals. But by being aware of signals and using these techniques, your chances for sales success increase dramatically.

> One word of caution in closing, do not underestimate the power of silence: **Once you have asked for the sale, be quiet.** Resist the temptation to speak! More sales people have talked themselves out of sales than have won a customer with extra "conversation." Let silence work for you.

After you have asked, it's the customer's responsibility to answer. If there is a long silence, it usually means your customer is seriously thinking about your offer. A negative response typically comes quickly. Don't think of closing as pushing a customer into buying something. If you are convinced that your product meets all their requirements, then getting them to commit to a purchase may be doing them a big favor, actually keeping them from procrastinating, or helping them be more productive, and let them move on to other projects.

Chapter Nine

Building Block #7: Follow-Through and Begin Again

Strengthening Customer's Commitment to You and Your Organization.

This sales success skill, entitled "Follow Through & Begin Again" appears at the end of the Consultative Sales Skill training. However, it is important to understand that these concepts can be applied at any time during a customer call and at any time during your sales call cycle contact with customers. The **customer call** refers to the immediate customer contact and the **sales call cycle** refers to the continued relationship that you build with your customers, both initiating Outbound prospecting calls and follow-up calls and responding to Inbound calls.

Let's begin with the concept of **"Sales is Service and Service is Sales."**

1. What does this concept mean to each of you?

2. And, how might you currently be using or how might you plan to use this "Sales is Service and Service is Sales" approach to "add-value" in the mind of your customer?

3. What would you say is the central ingredient of your success with each of your "regular" customers?

4. How can you leverage off of the success of your existing "regular" customers?

5. What do you need to do to continue to strengthen both your sales and service resources and skills?

Let's now consider the importance of "**Reinforcing Your Sales Consultant Role and Thanking the Customer.**" **When you fulfill the role of Sales Consultant, you provide information and service to your customer, thereby "Adding-Value".....**

When you conclude a call with your customer or thank your customer for their order you should ensure them of the following:

1. You understand the needs of your customer

2. Your customer understands the **value and benefits** of your products and services **AND OF DOING BUSINESS WITH YOU!**

3. Your customer knows how you will continue to service his or her account.

NOTE: The above three "value-adding" considerations apply to you and your customer whether or not you make the immediate sale. Your professionalism and thoroughness will establish a positive foundation for building a relationship with your customer during future customer call contacts.

Some Strategies for "Adding-Value".....

How can you demonstrate to your customer that you understand their needs?

How can you communicate to them the value and benefits of your products and services?

On a personal note, how does your customer know the value and benefits of DOING BUSINESS WITH YOU?

What are several ways which you, as a sales pro, can position yourself as a resource to your customer for continuing to service his or her account?

Name three things that you can do to prove to your customer that you have their long-term interests in mind.

In order to build a long-term business "partnership" with your customer, you have to demonstrate through your words and, more importantly, actions that you have **their** best interests in mind (and not necessarily yours.)

Let's now consider the importance of **"Addressing Issues Promptly and Asking for Referrals."** It has been said that when something goes wrong in the eyes of the customer, we can be assured of one thing....WE HAVE THEIR ATTENTION...and what we do from that point forward will MAKE or BREAK our future business relationship with them.

So.........When a "Moment of Regret" has occurred for one of our customers, you may be on the receiving end of their call to your company. The first thing to do is to recognize that the "situation" that the customer is calling about may have nothing to do with you. However, now it is your opportunity to try to turn that "Moment of Regret" into a "Moment of Delight." This process is called **Service Recovery** and basically it means that your role, interest, concern and attention to detail is of utmost importance to the customer at this critical stage.

Following are three levels of customer dissatisfaction which should assist you in understanding the customer's perspective and their need to have the issue addressed and resolved in a timely manner.

"Moments of Regret" and Degrees of Dissatisfaction

Level #1: Bothered- Customers are bothered when service falls short of their
            expectations, disappoints them slightly or surprises them negatively,
            but does not cause inconvenience.

Level #2: Irritated- Customers become irritated when they are annoyed by
            poor service, somewhat inconvenienced or have lost time but not
            money.

Level #3: Abused-Customers feel abused when they are grossly inconvenienced, have
            lost time and money, are personally insulted or unfairly treated,
            or are made angry or upset.

> When handling dissatisfied customers, it is important to determine to what degree they are dissatisfied. The more upset, the greater and faster your efforts will have to be to correct the situation.

-

What customer characteristics help you to distinguish the **difference** between a direct and task focused customer AND a dissatisfied customer?

What are some methods you use to determine how concerned or dissatisfied your customer might be about a particular issue?

Following is a strategy and coping skills for addressing customer issues. To practice, think about a "customer dissatisfaction scenario" and perhaps team up with another sales person to role-play the situation using the L.I.S.T.E.N. approach.

Remember that the acronym **L.I.S.T.E.N.** is being used to remind you that it is important to listen with the intent to understand...before responding with your perspective.

L: Let the Customer talk without interruption. (Handle the person first).

I: Identify their Need, Concern or Problem.
   (Paraphrase their situation and Address their problem.)

S: Strategize with the customer Win/Win Options, Choices & Alternatives.

T: Take notes on what you hear, acknowledge their situation
   and agree on a Win/Win Solution.

E: Empathize with your customer.

N: Never forget that you are the key to your Customer's Satisfaction

Asking for Referrals..... Referrals both inside and outside your customer's company are the **lifeblood** of both your and your company's business success. Let's discuss the signals to watch for in order to know that your customer would be willing to provide you with referrals, both inside and outside of their company.

Asking for Customer Referrals Both Inside and Outside the Company:

1. What do you say to the customer when they say....."I buy the software products for this location, but someone else purchases the corporate license agreements"................

2. What do you say to the customer when they say...."I'm just ordering these products...... they are not for me."

3. What do you say when you ask them a question about the purchase they are placing and they can't answer them?

4. When you know you have a satisfied customer whom you are speaking with, what do you say to them to encourage them to provide you with several names of others within the company who also might benefit from your services?

5. When you know you have both a satisfied and loyal customer whom you have built up a relationship with, what do you say to them to encourage them to provide you with several names of others outside the company who also might benefit from your services?

Common Problems and Mistakes to Avoid

Here are some examples of problems and mistakes which derail Account Executives from obtaining the level of performance that they desire. Learning from these pitfalls will enable you to excel. Knowing **what not to do** becomes as important as knowing **what to do**. Here are some tips...

Five Death Sentences to a Sale

_____• **Not Reaching the Right Person.** All too often, an Account Executive will talk to the first person who listens. Even if that person wants to help, he may not have the authority to make any commitments. Unfortunately, this is generally discovered when the Account Executive tries to close and hears "I need to take this to..." or "You'll have to talk to..." Be sure to qualify the person you're talking to. Can she make the decision? If not, who does? It saves a lot of sales time to find out up front in your contacts with prospects.

_____•**Talking About Features Instead of Benefits.**
The second death sentence occurs for one of two reasons: excessive enthusiasm, or ignorance of your customer and his needs.   Features enable a customer to enjoy a product's benefit, <u>but a feature by itself doesn't mean anything.</u> We have to **translate product and service features (characteristics or facts of a product/service) into benefits (the value received or "What is the advantage to me")** for our prospects and customers. In our excitement to make the sale, we might assume that our customers know the benefit to them. CONFIRM IT!   Spell it out in their language, not yours.

_____• **Winning Arguments.** All of us have at some time regretted what we said. It may have been in anger or it may have just been a mistake. Nowhere is it more costly than in sales. Even if your prospect is difficult to deal with or upsets you with some careless or thoughtless remark, don't jeopardize the sale for a few minutes satisfaction by starting an argument or making an emotional point. Control your emotions.

_____ • **Not Asking for the Sale.** People rarely tell each other how they want to be treated—but they demonstrate it. Your customer may have listened to your whole presentation, objected a few times and is now satisfied that your product/service will satisfy his need. Will she ask you if she can buy it? Hardly! Since the majority of our communication involves signs and signals, that is probably how you will be informed. Your prospect lets you know it is OK to ask for the sale. If you don't ask, your customer won't volunteer to buy. What's more, she starts to lose interest or confidence in you as you continue to avoid the close. All too soon, you've talked yourself out of a sale without ever asking.

_____ • **Talking Too Much.** The last death sentence ties in very closely with "Not Asking." Some Account Executives mistake silence for acceptance. As long as the customer is quiet, they keep talking. What may actually be happening is that the customer is waiting for his chance to signal the Account Executive to close. As the Account Executive talks on, that "window of opportunity" begins to close and the customer begins to cool off. Be aware of the buying signals that we discussed earlier and always be willing to ask for the sale.

The Most Common Mistakes. The five death sentences almost always result in lost sales.

However, there are other mistakes an Account Executive can make that create trouble or failure. Although they may not be quite as serious, they should be avoided. Here are some to avoid:

_____ • **Dropping the Price.** Many Account Executives think that lower prices automatically mean higher demand and more sales. This is not the case. More often than not, price is associated with the quality of your product and its perceived value. By automatically dropping your price at the slightest hint of a price objection, you send a signal back that says: My product/service isn't as good as I said it was; since I was wrong on this item, I may be wrong on other items that I have told you. Now you have two credibility problems—one with your product and one with yourself. You are better off sticking to the value of your product and not compromising it or yourself in the process.

_____ • **Announcing Instead of Selling.** If you are very knowledgeable about your product (and you should be), you can be guilty of making that deadly assumption—that your customer can translate new features of your product into new benefits for himself or his business. When you make that assumption, you just announce the new product/features rather than starting with a whole new sales process. Make sure your prospect knows how those new features are going to help him.

_____ • **Hard Selling Instead of Need Selling.** We all have an image in our minds of the fast talking, hard-selling sales person that nobody wants to talk to. Today's customer's are more educated, more sophisticated, and not likely to be intimidated or convinced by that style. They are looking for sales people who respect their wishes, are a reputable source of information, can help them with their problems and needs, and have their business success as top priority. In return, they will place their orders where they feel most secure. Show your prospects and customers how you can be a valuable appreciating resource to them by becoming a consultant to them and their business. Provide solutions which address and solve your customer's challenges and you will make the sale everytime.

_____ • **Failure to Follow-Through.** Hopefully, we have communicated through this training that every customer should be treated as an individual with specific preferences, needs, issues and challenges. One of the significant ways that an Account Executive can distinguish themselves is through effective follow-through actions. By demonstrating follow-through abilities, you send an important message to your customer. You communicate that you are a professional who meets all business commitments. You also reinforce the fact that you genuinely care about your customer and that caring goes beyond the quick sale.

Where Do You Go From Here?

I'd like to encourage you to keep your copy of the Consultative Selling workbook at your desk and USE IT as a REFERFENCE...BEFORE, DURING, and AFTER each of your sales calls. You should also consider using the workbook as a resource and focus for meetings with a colleague or two as you review and discuss concepts presented. Best of Luck as you continue to improve your ability to implement these consultative selling principles, skills, and techniques. Dan Duffy (daniel_duffy@comcast.net)

Handling Customer Objections (page 66) Answer Key:

1. S	2. O,S	3. Q	4. O	5. O
6. Q	7. Q	8. O	9. O, S	10. O